THIS BOOK

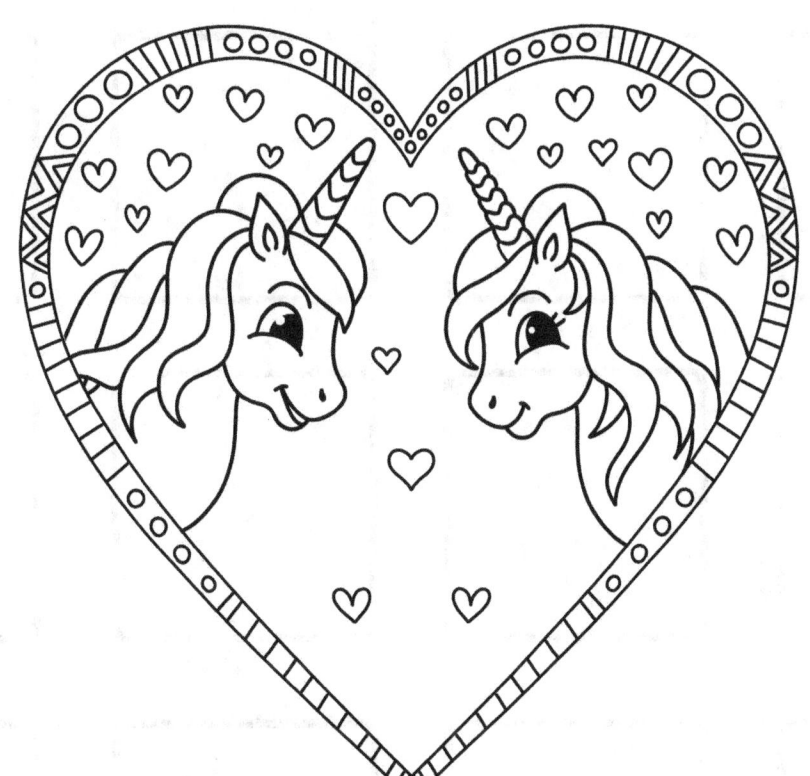

BELONGS TO

ooooooooooooooooooooooooooooooooo

ooooooooooooooooooooooooooooooooo

COLOR TEST

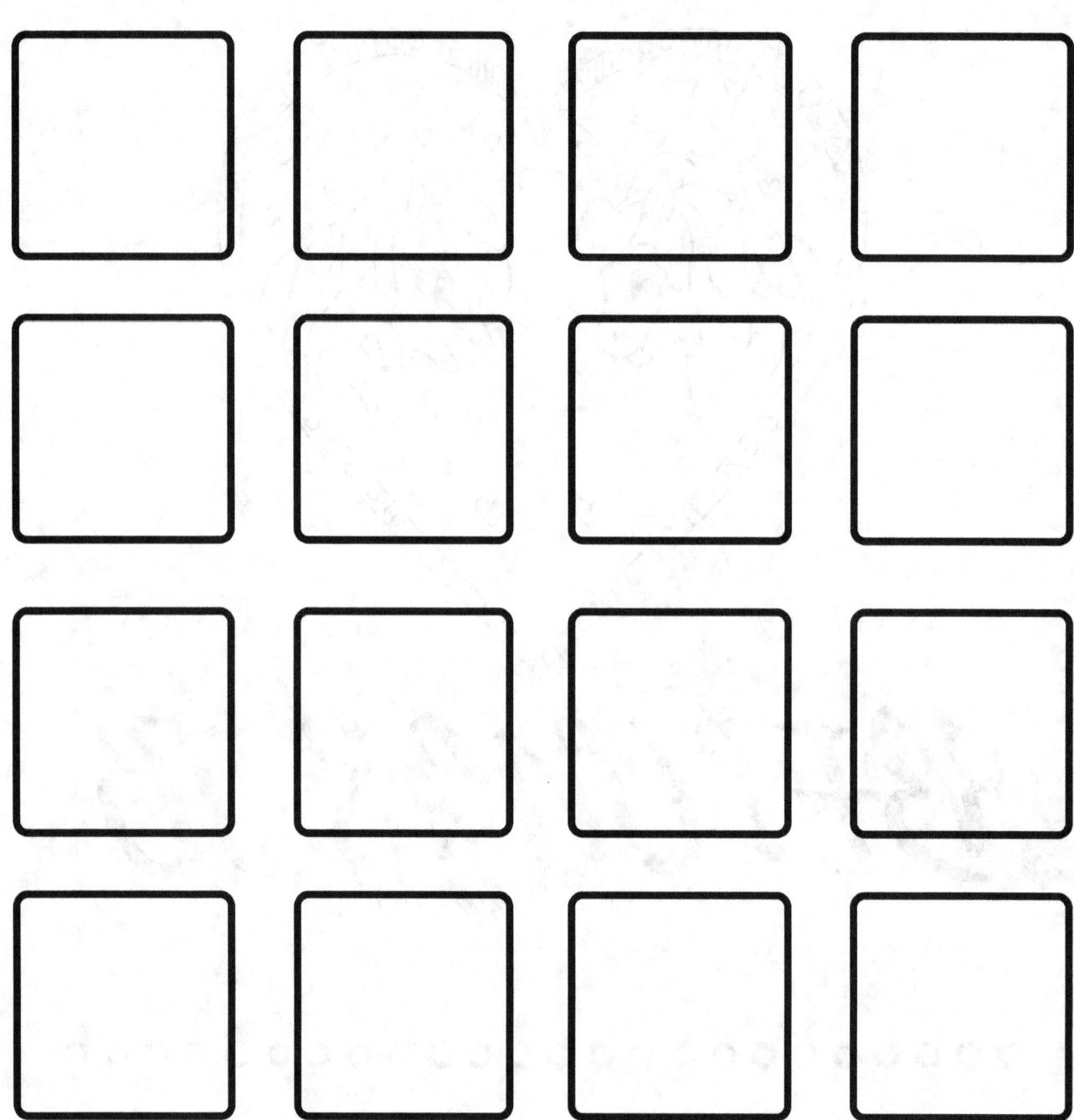

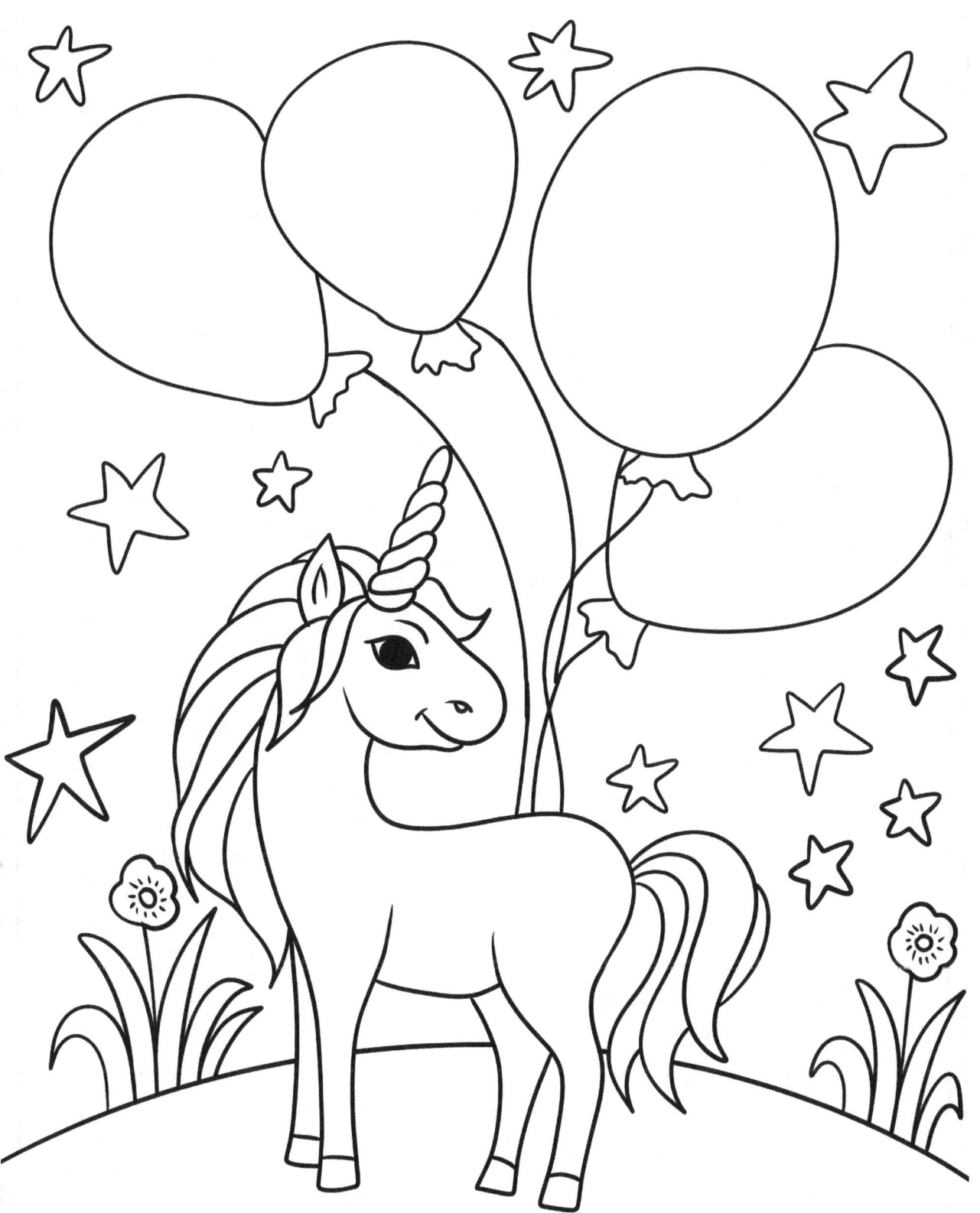

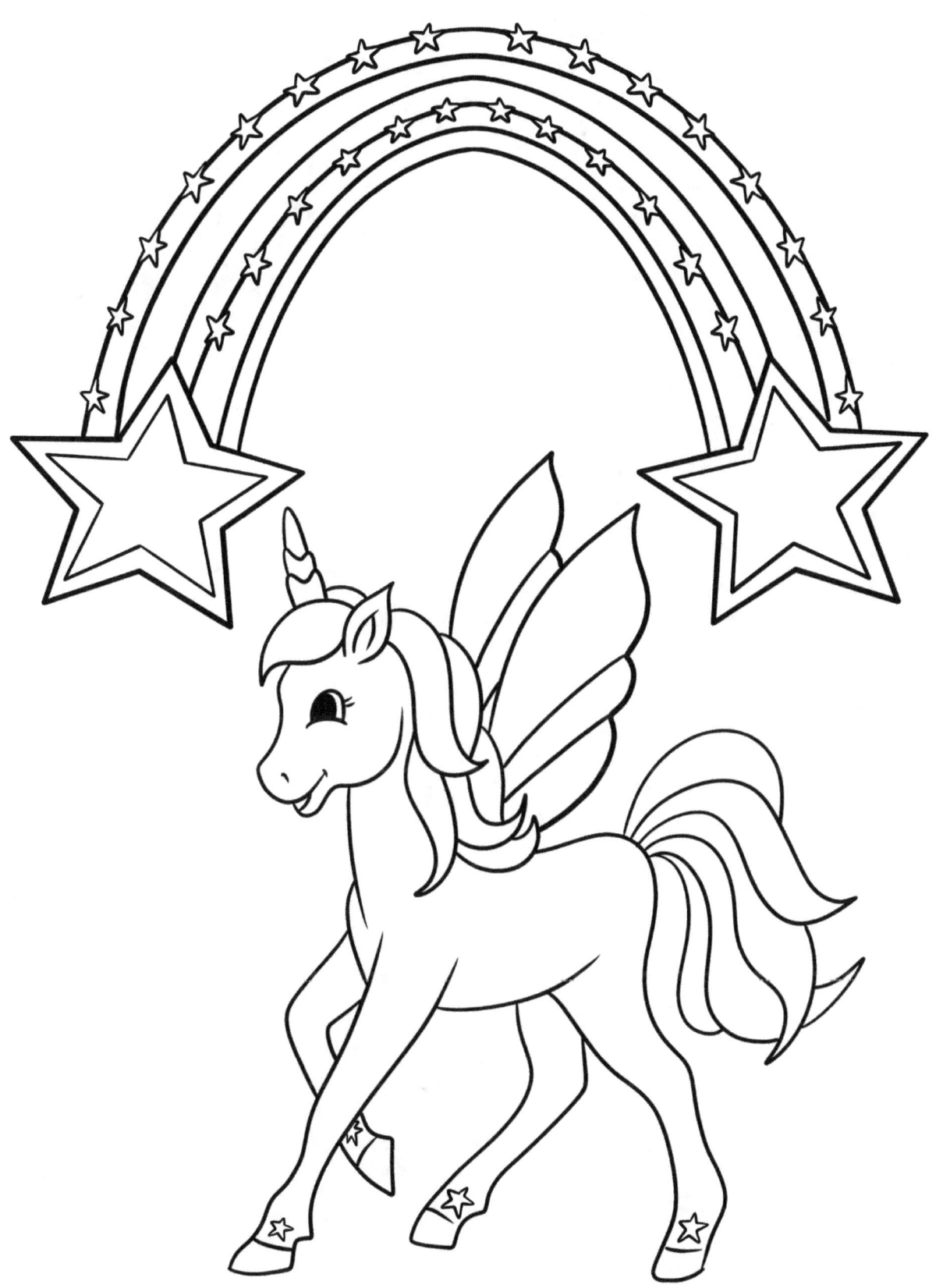

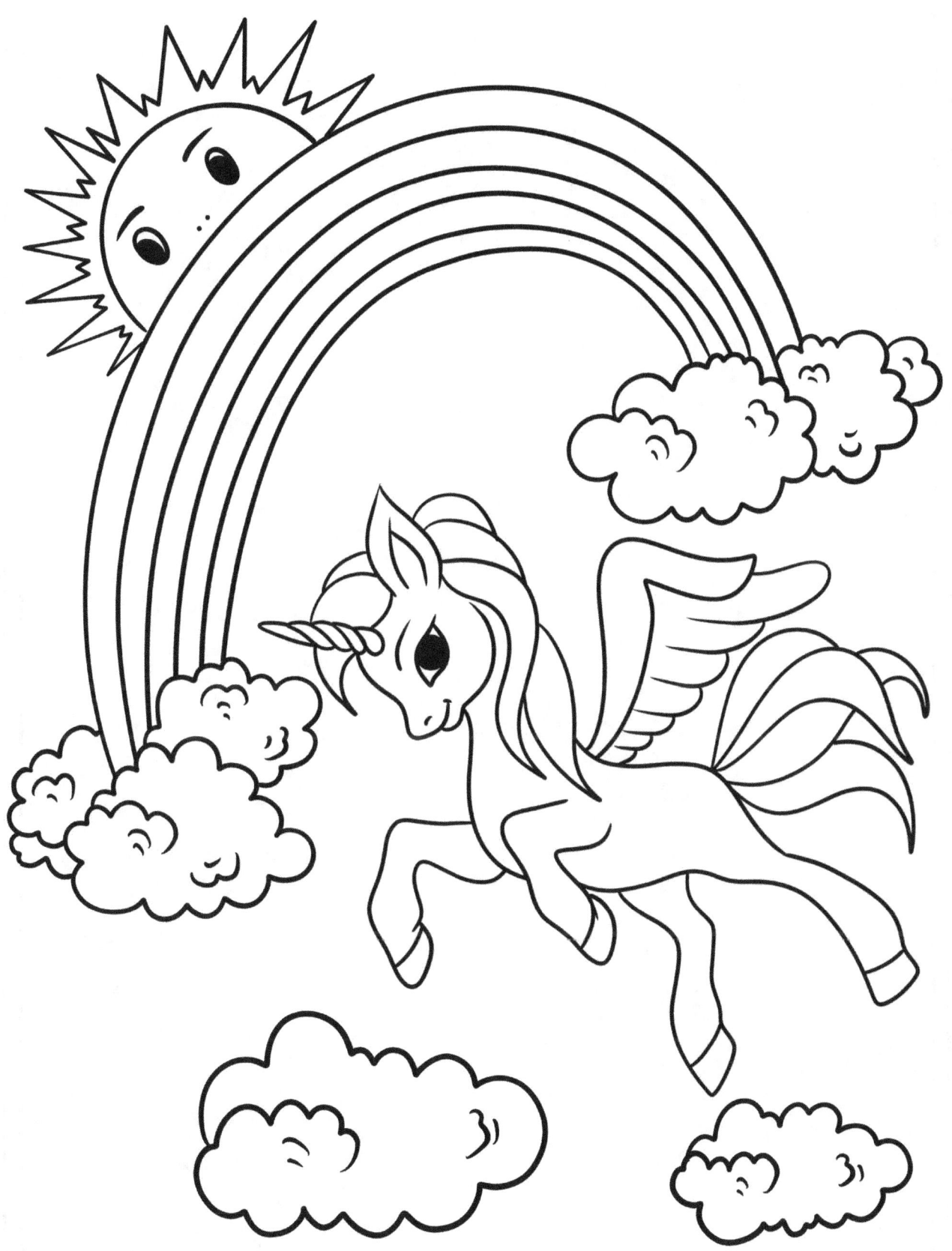

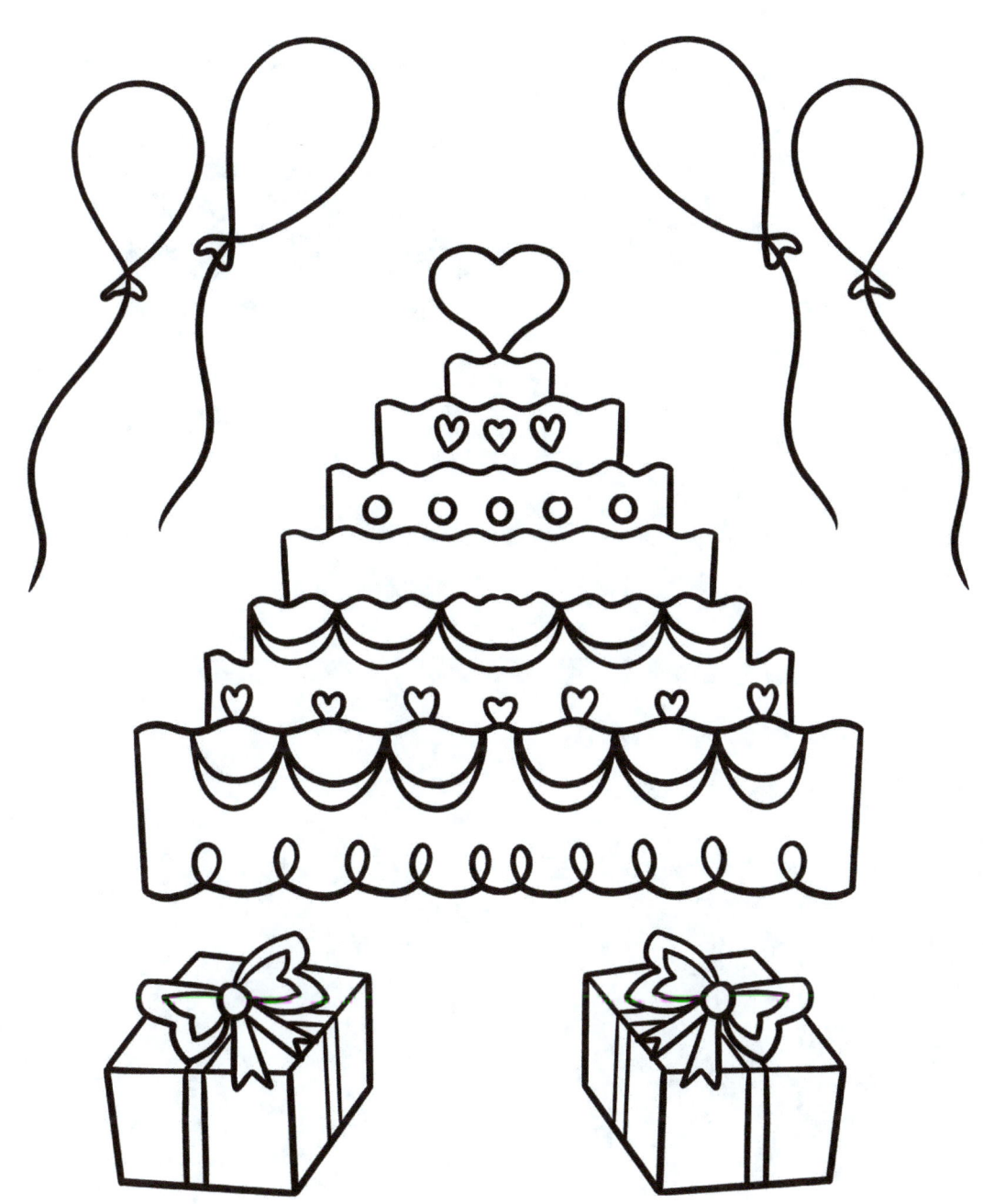

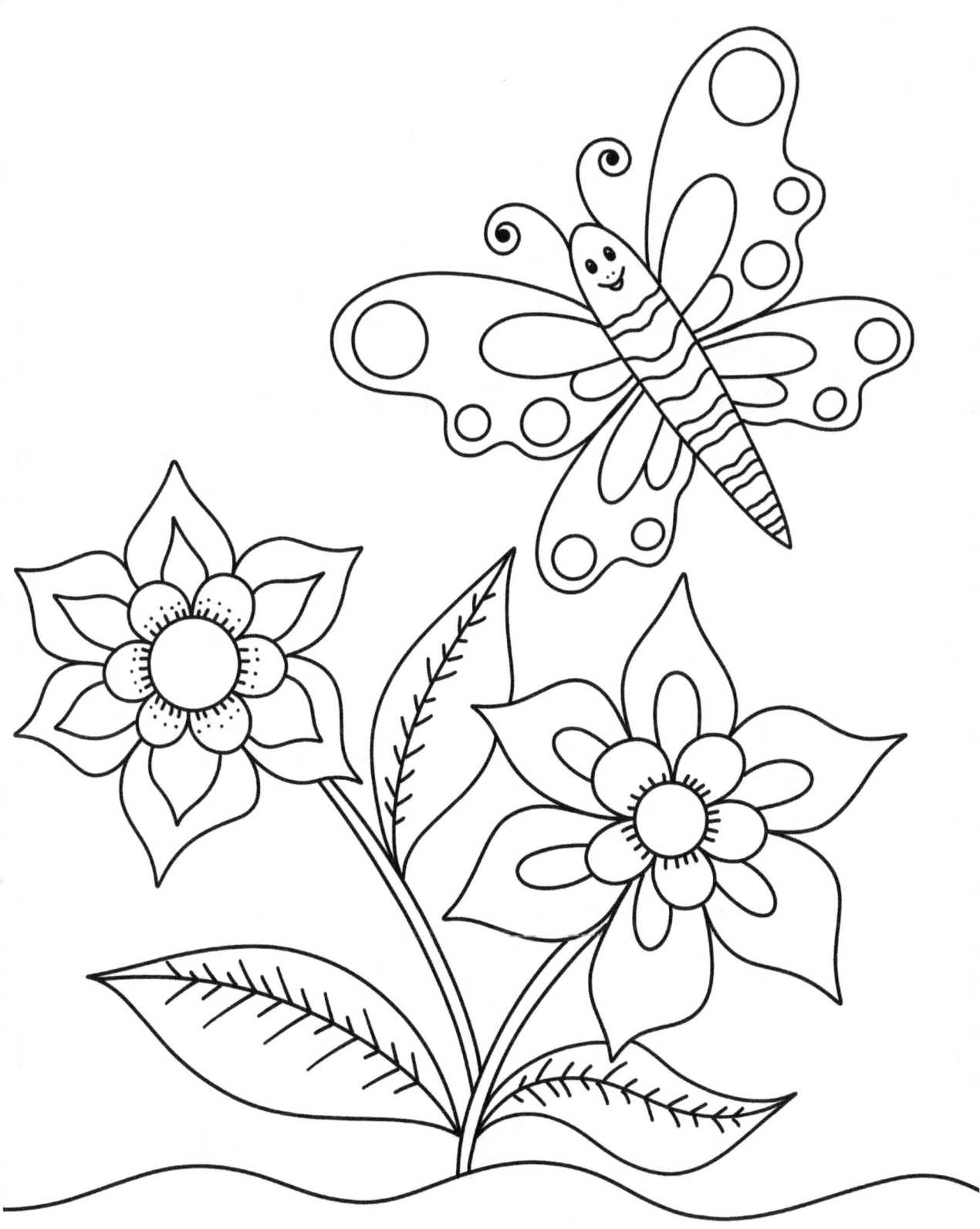

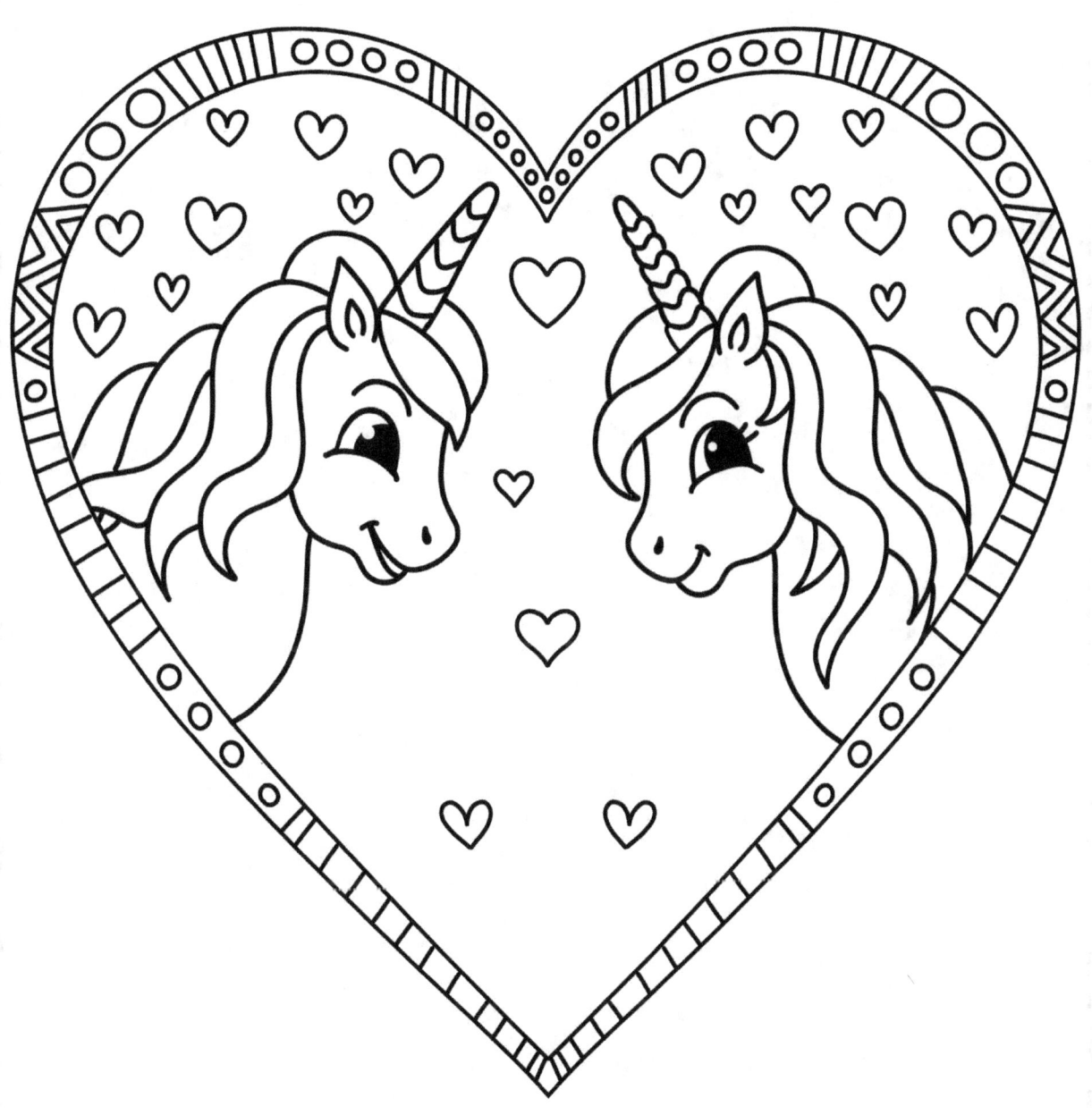

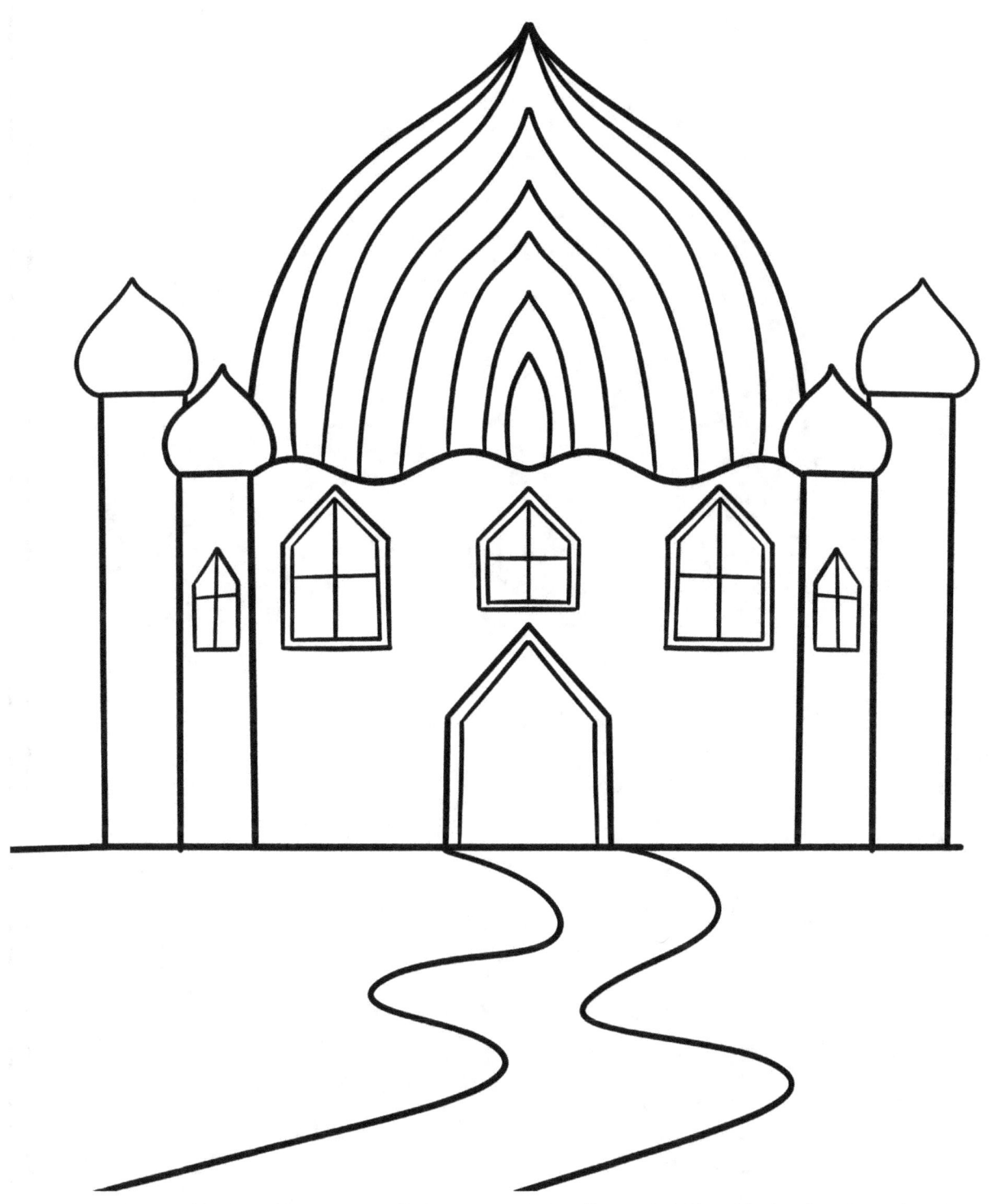

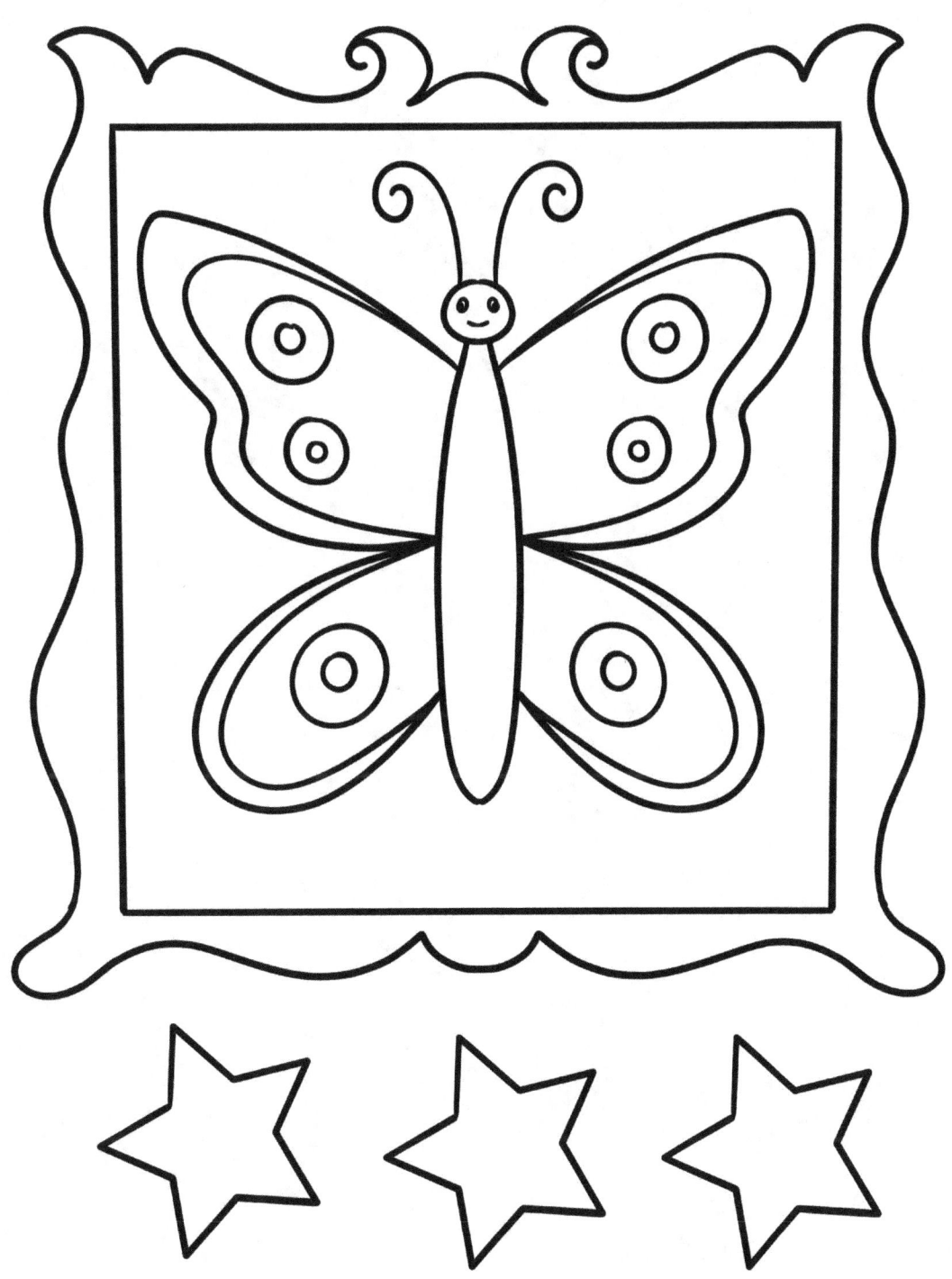

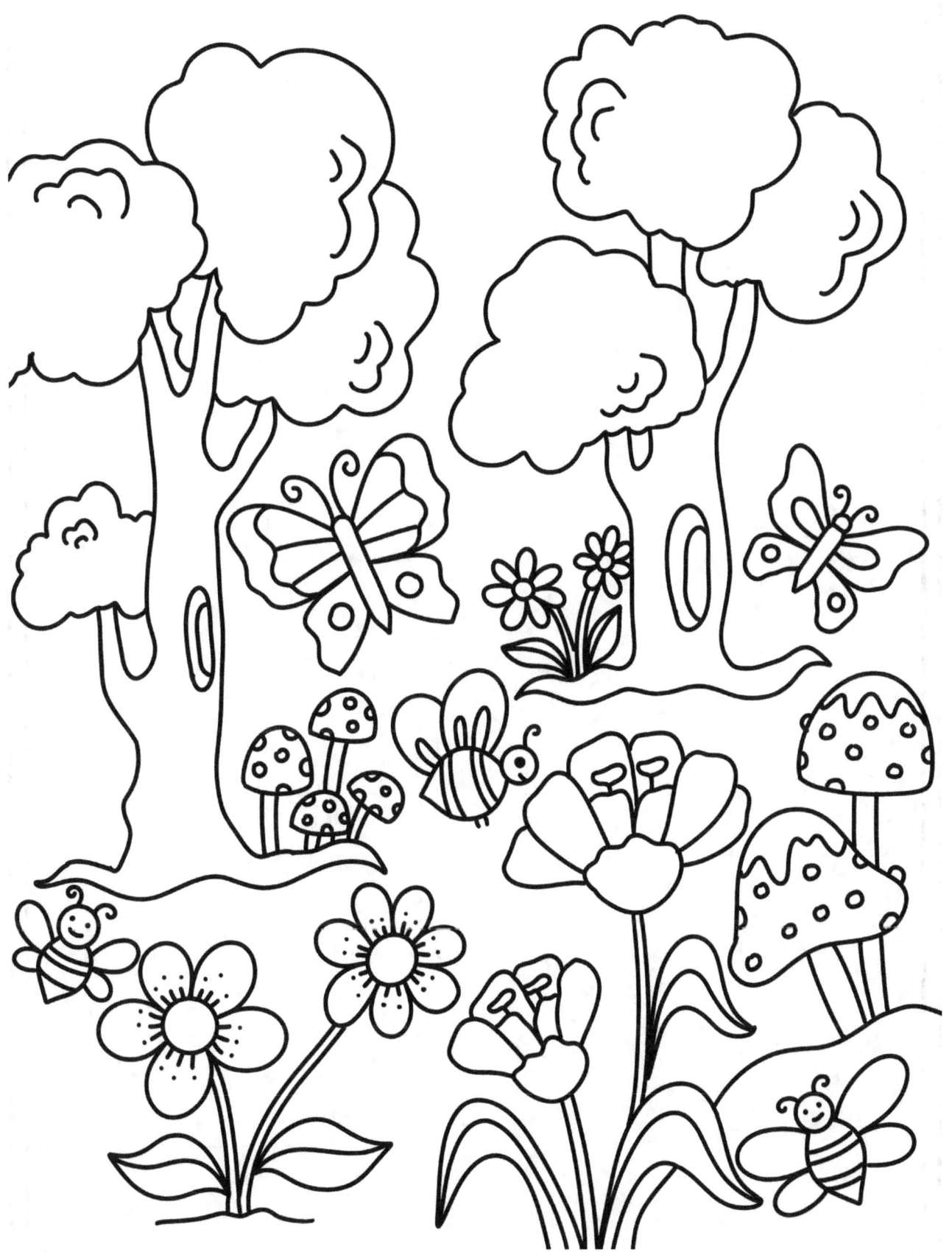

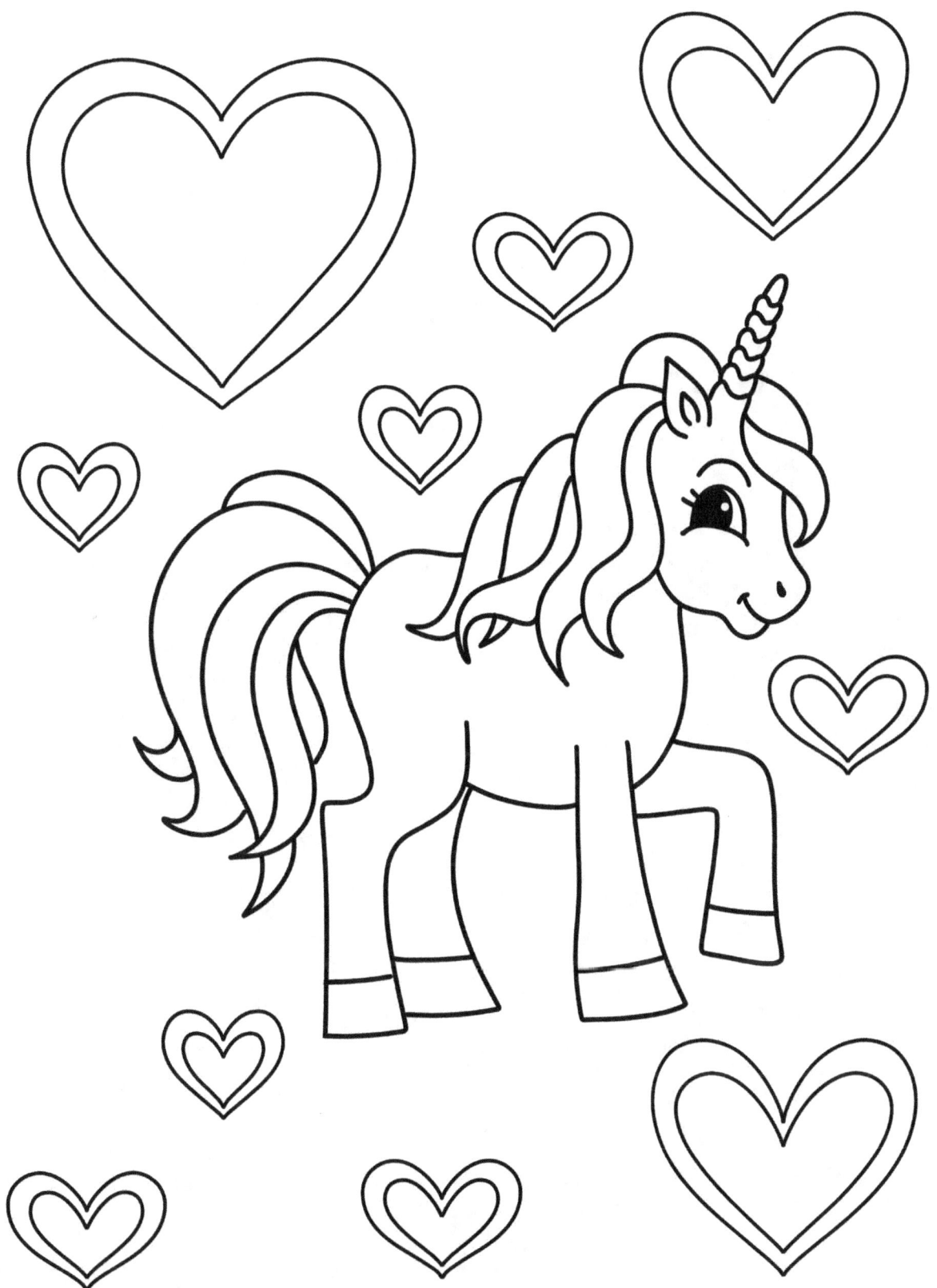

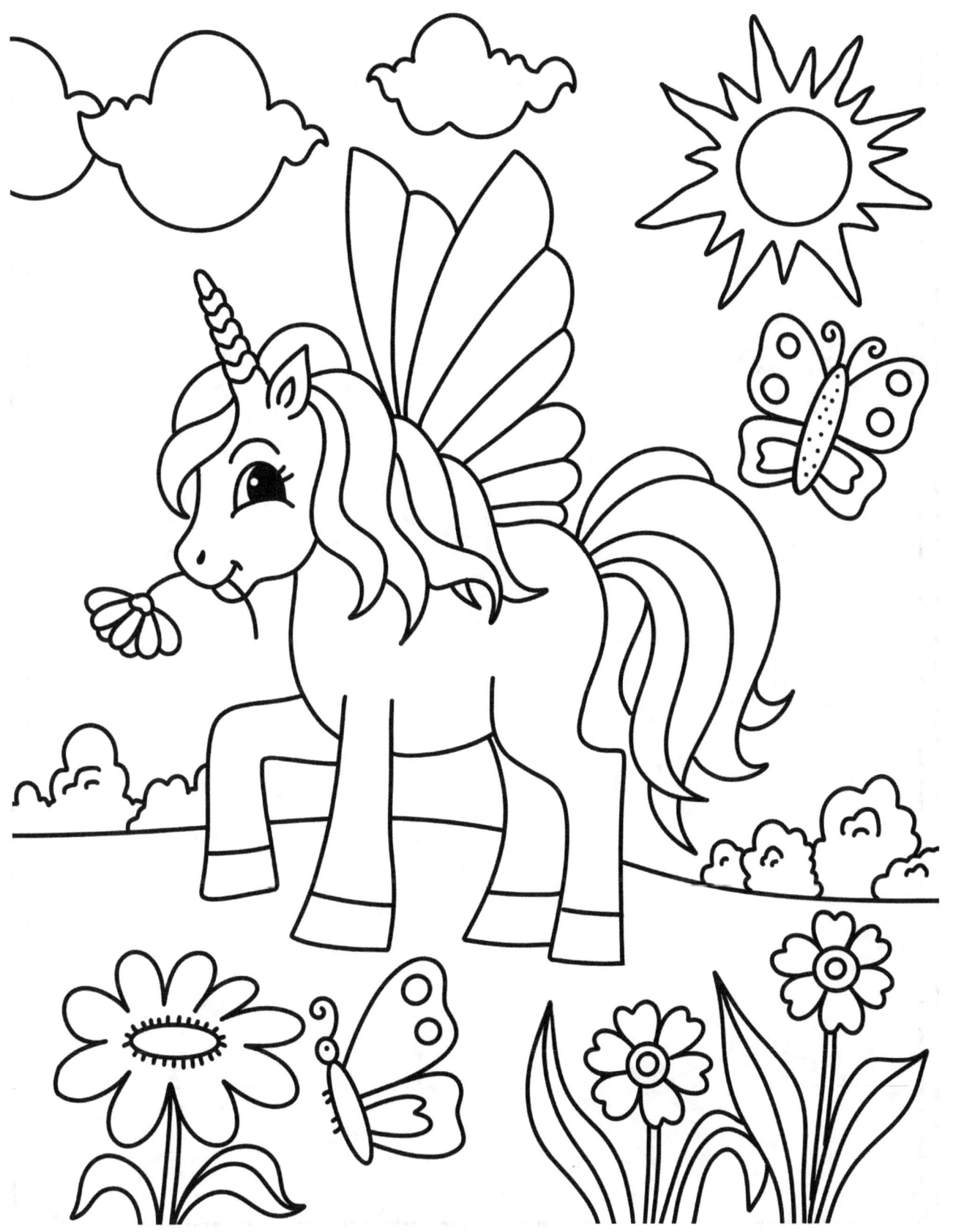

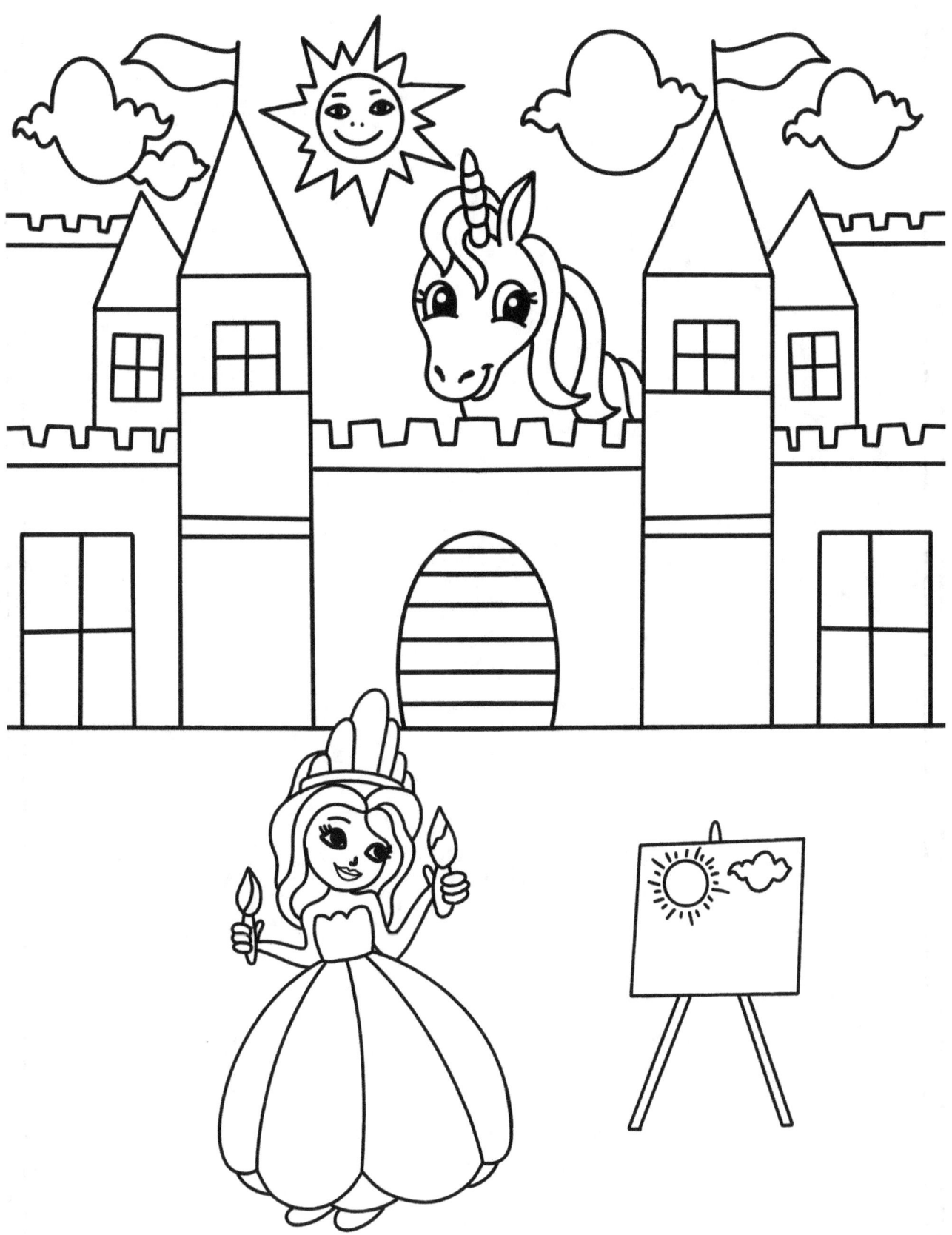

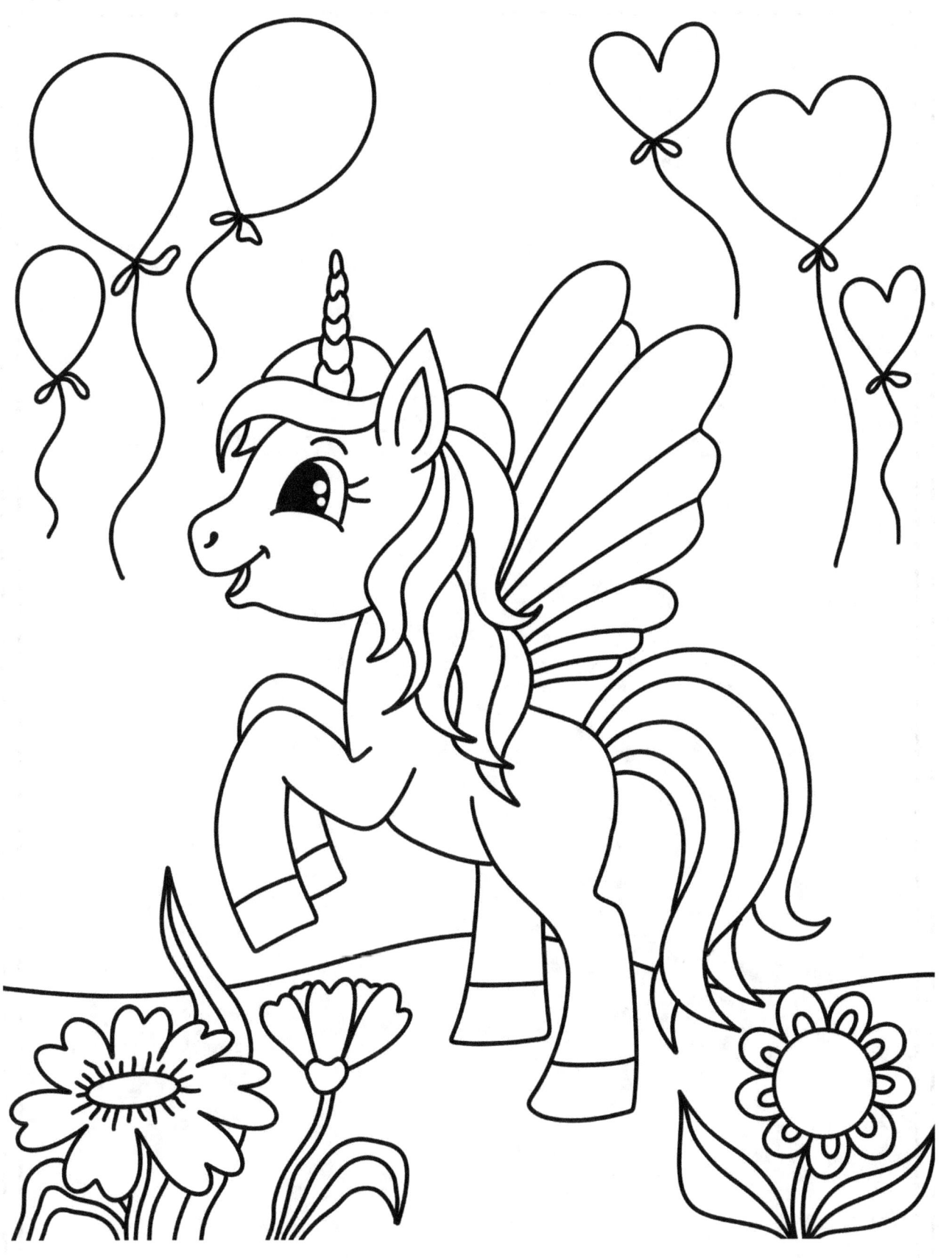

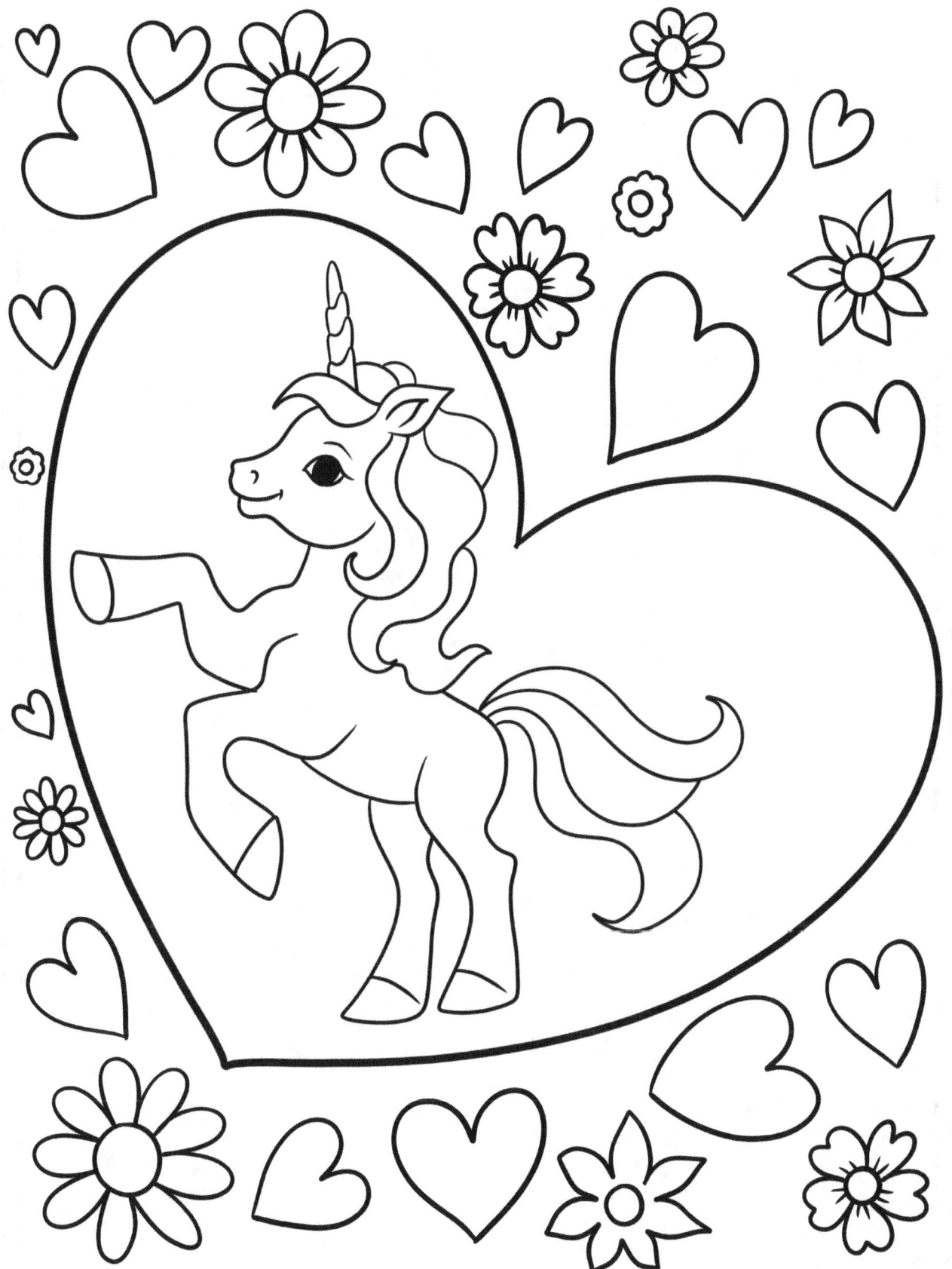

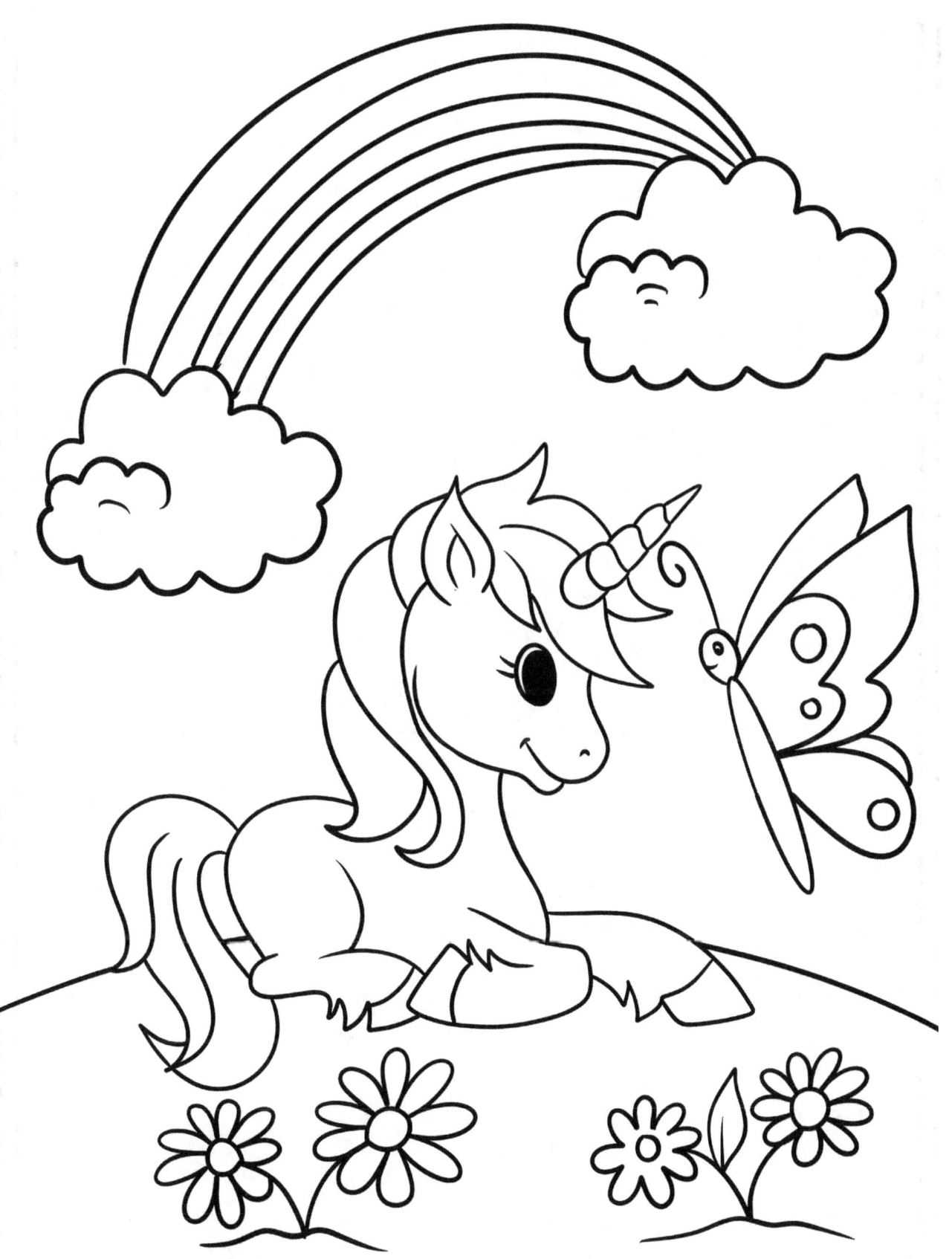

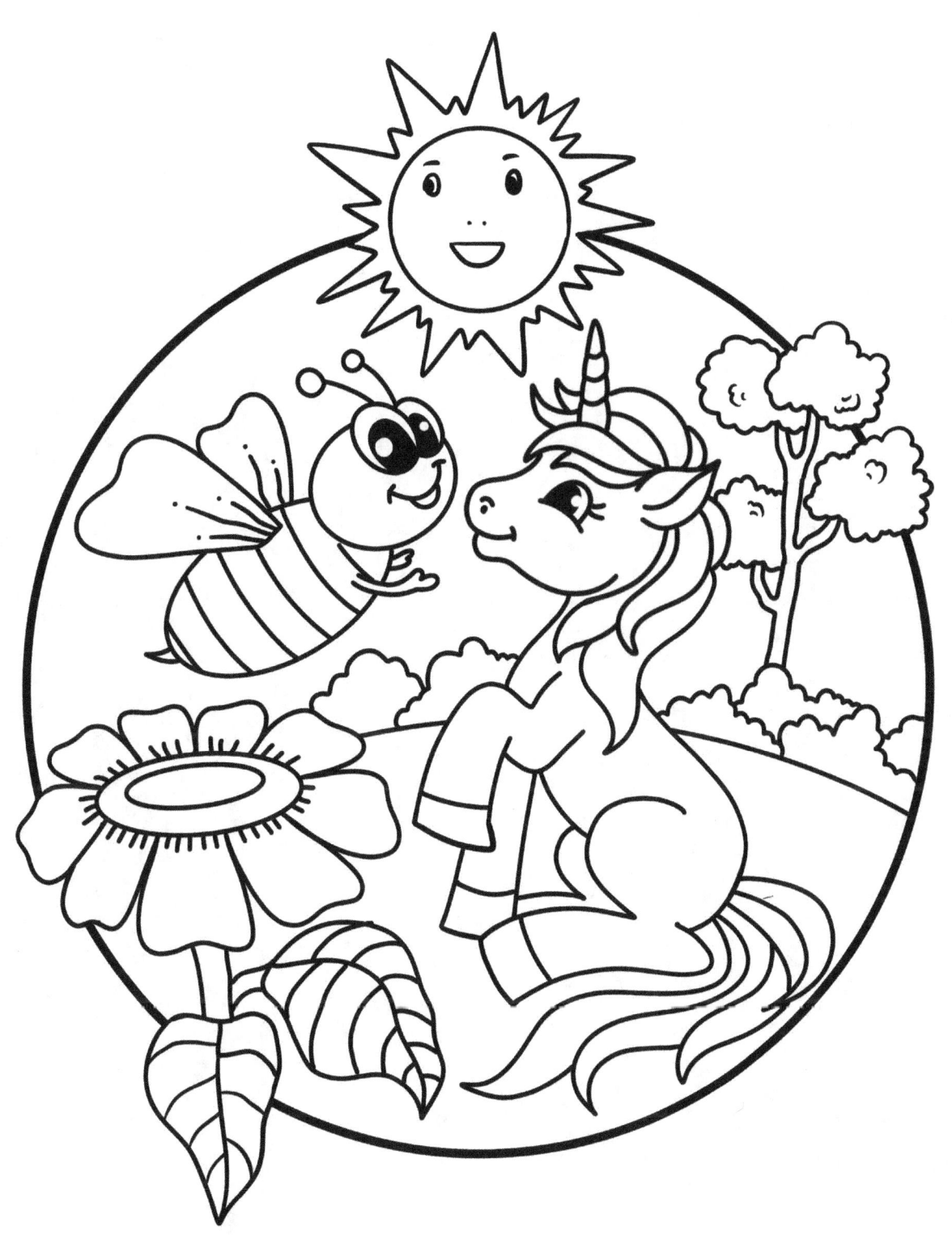

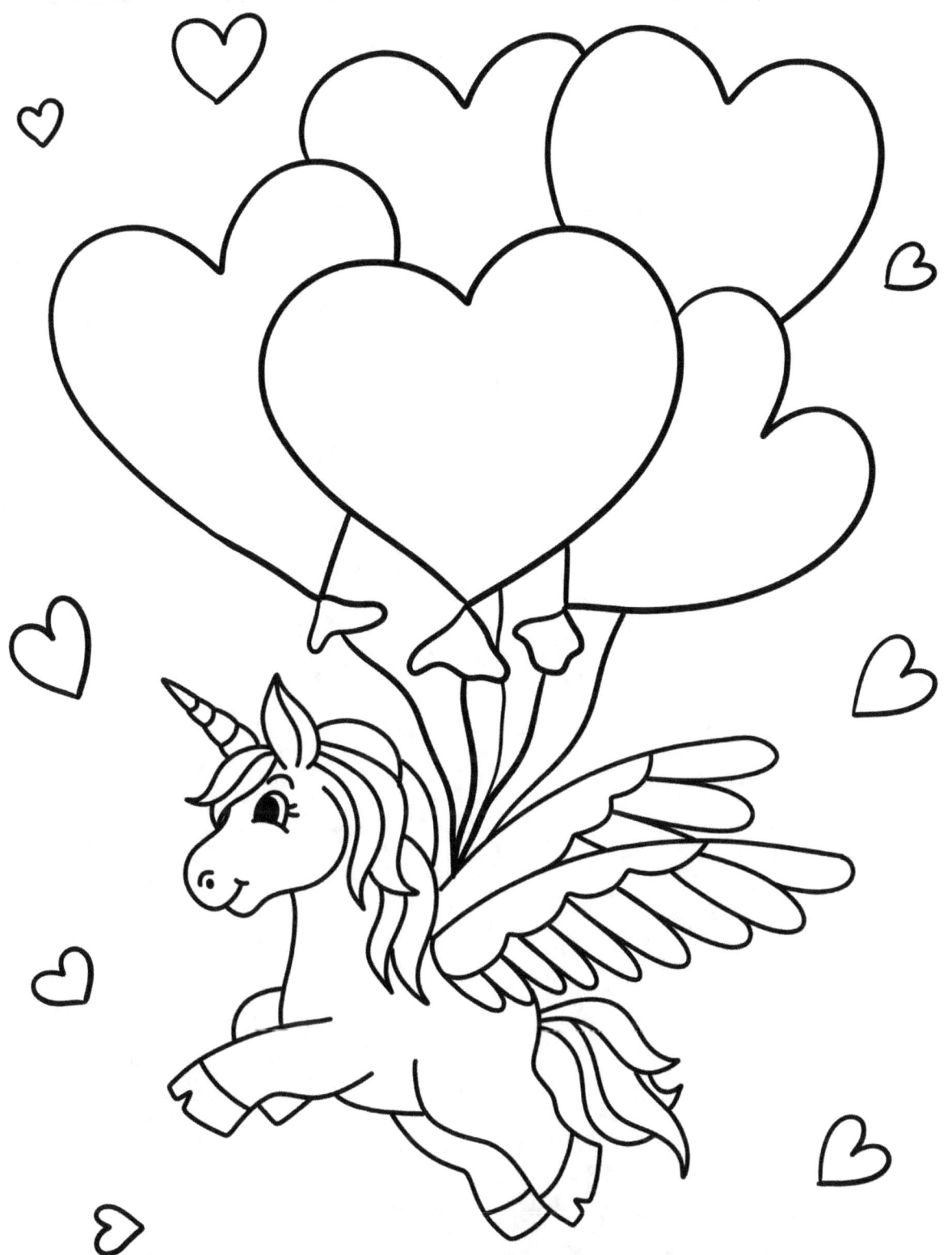

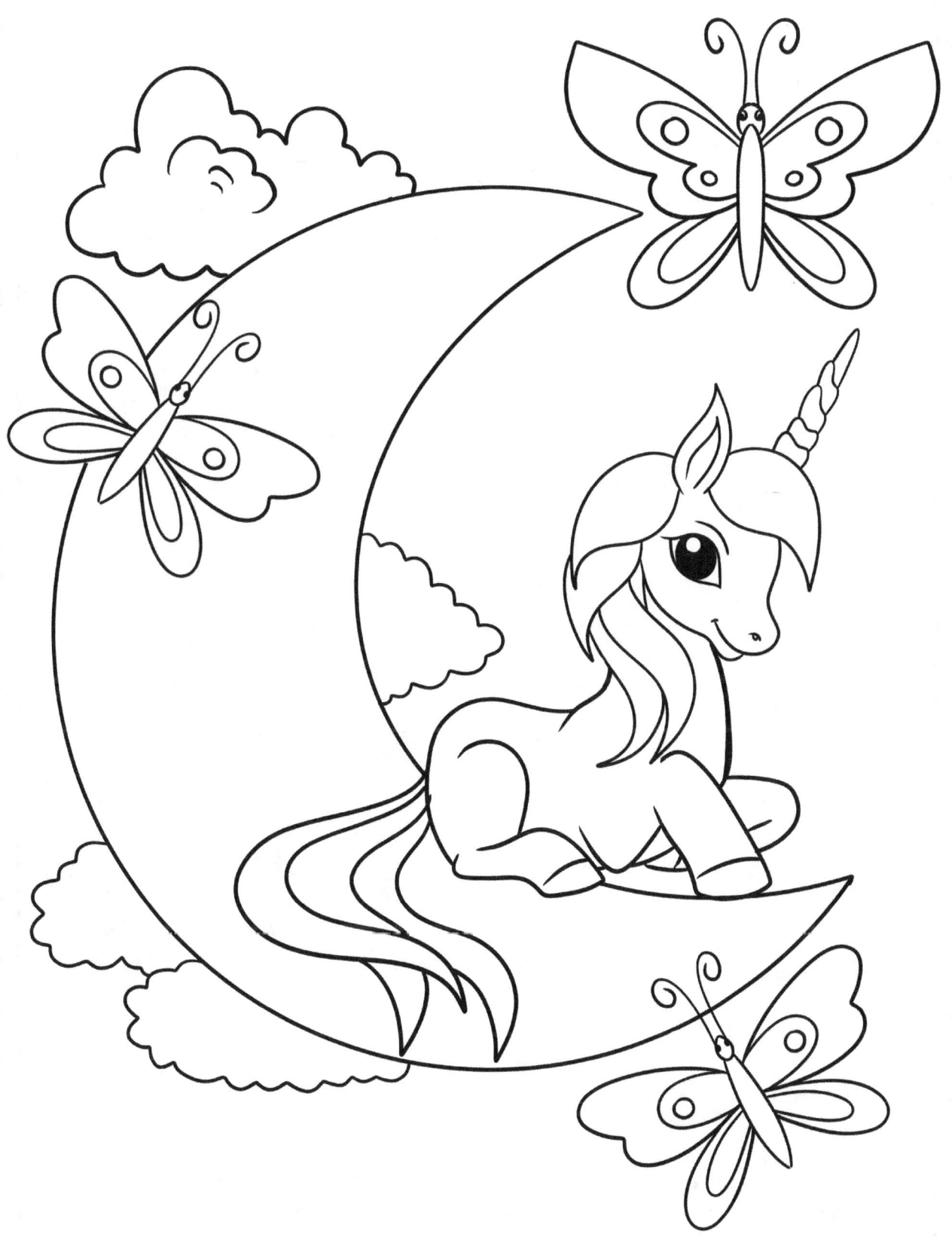

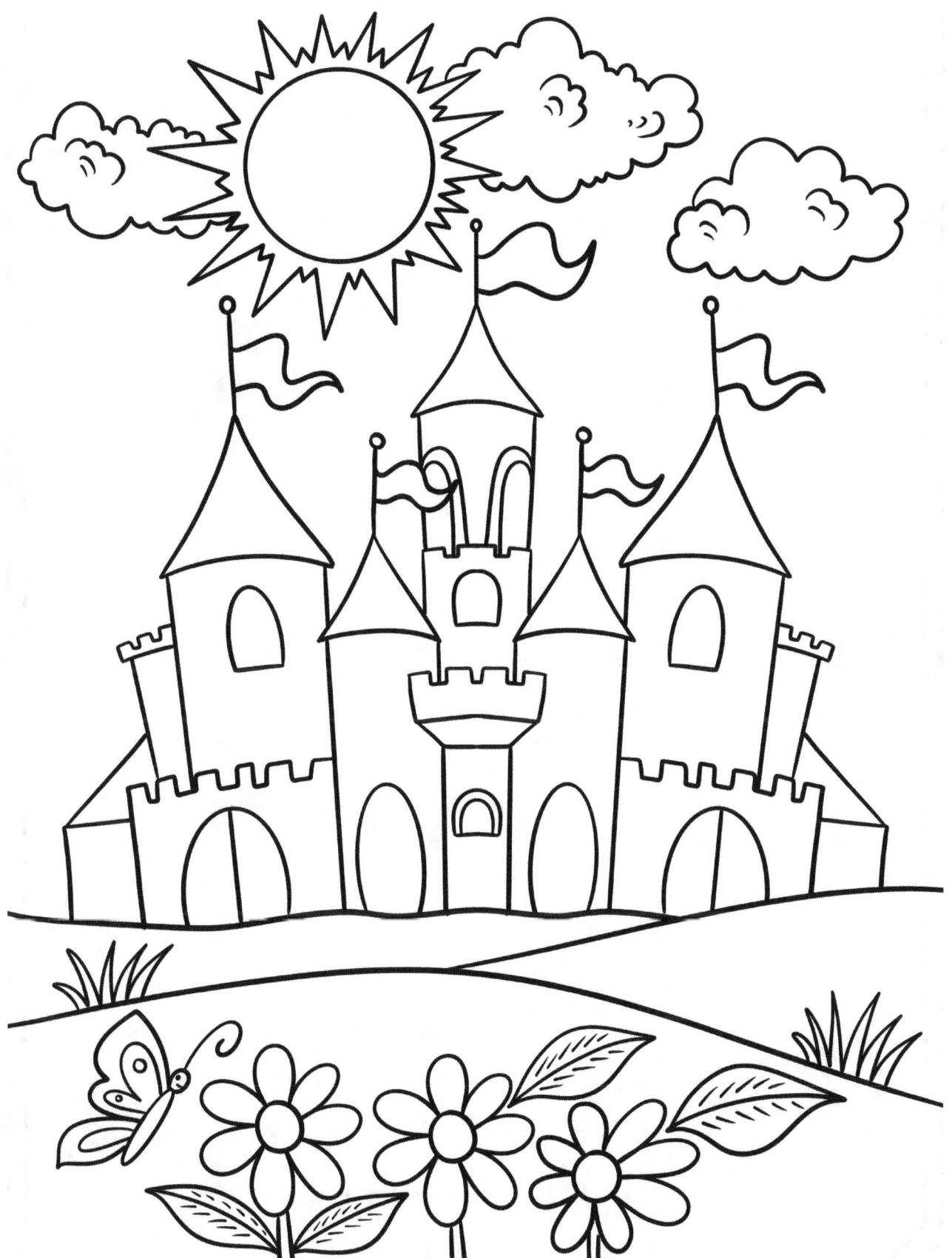

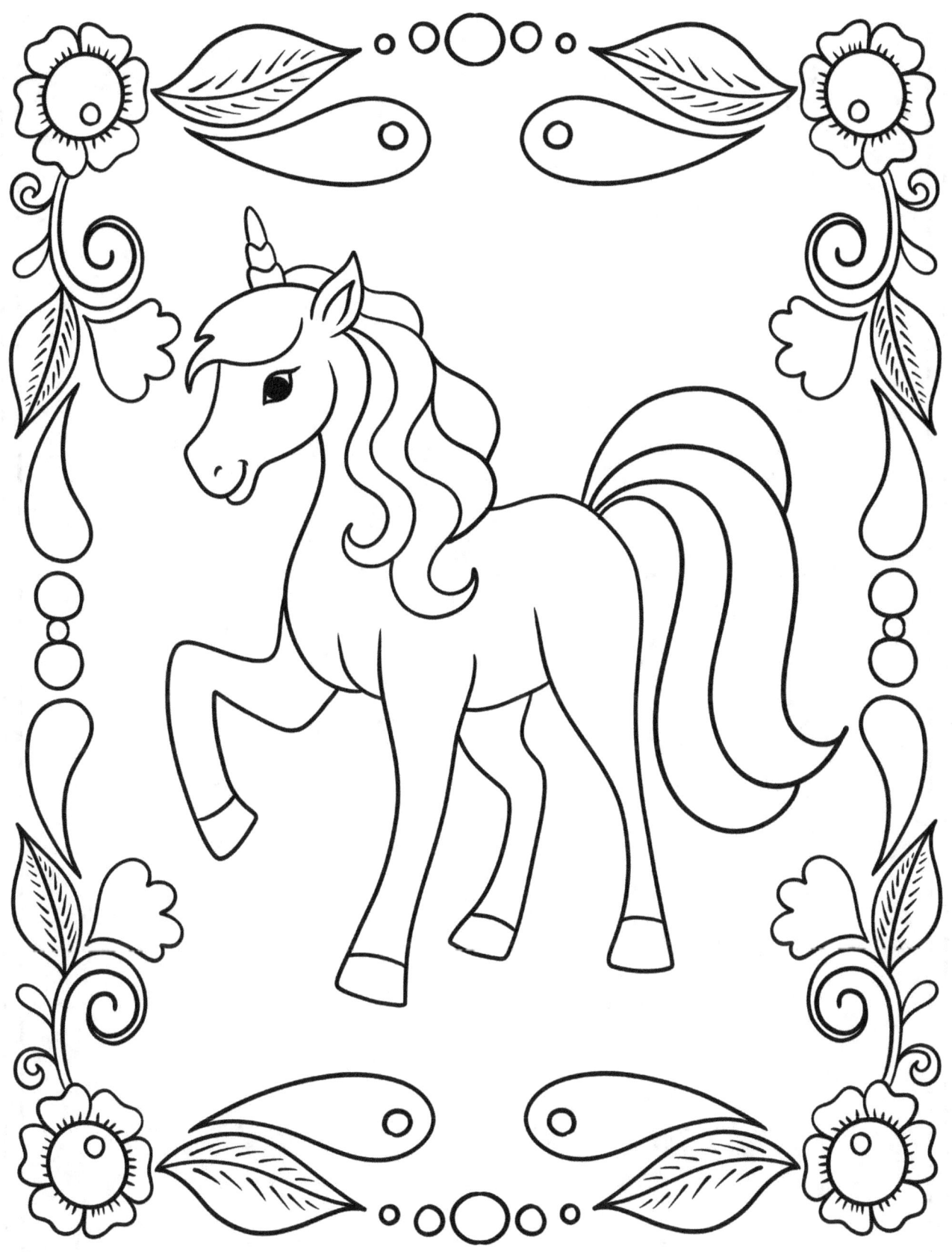

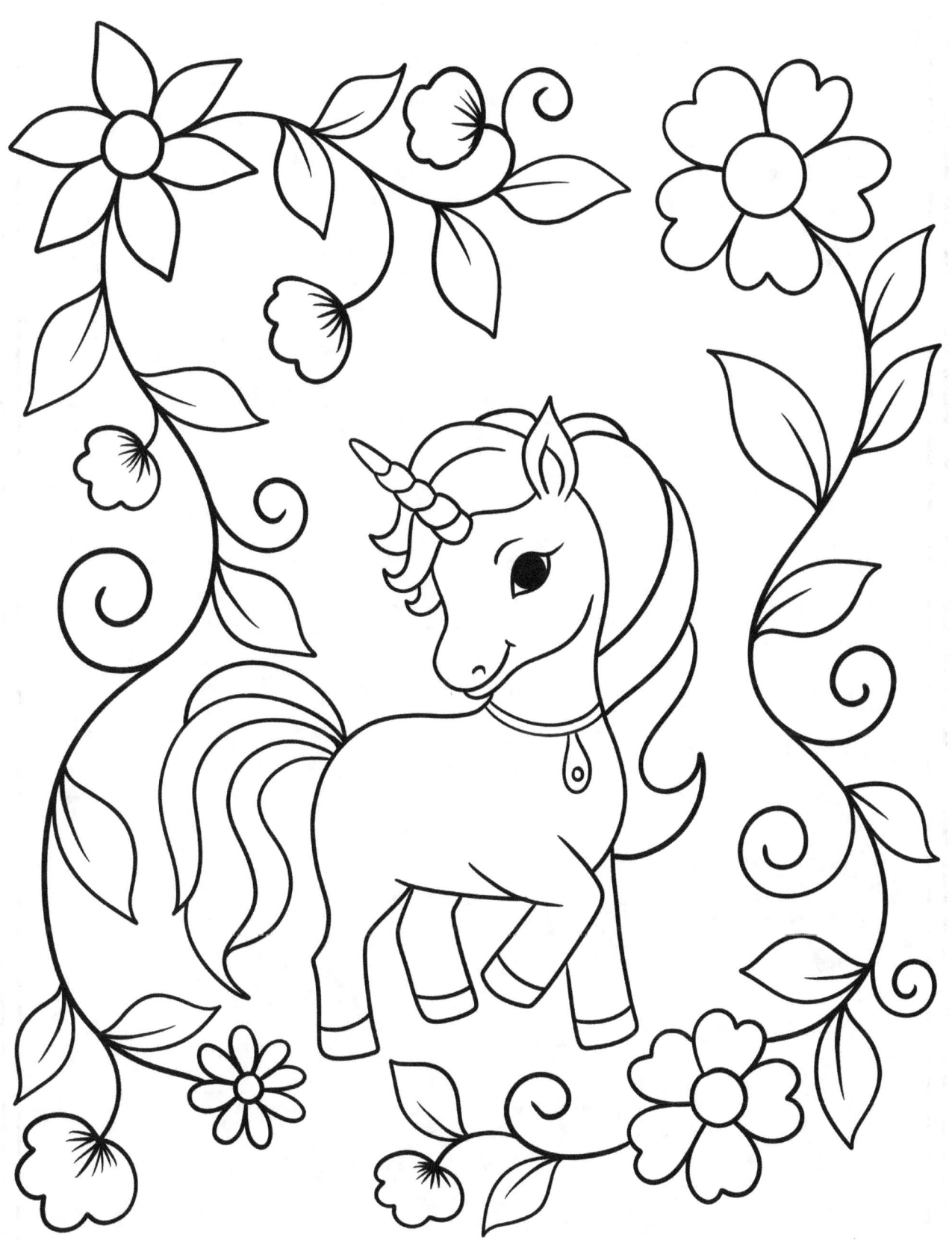

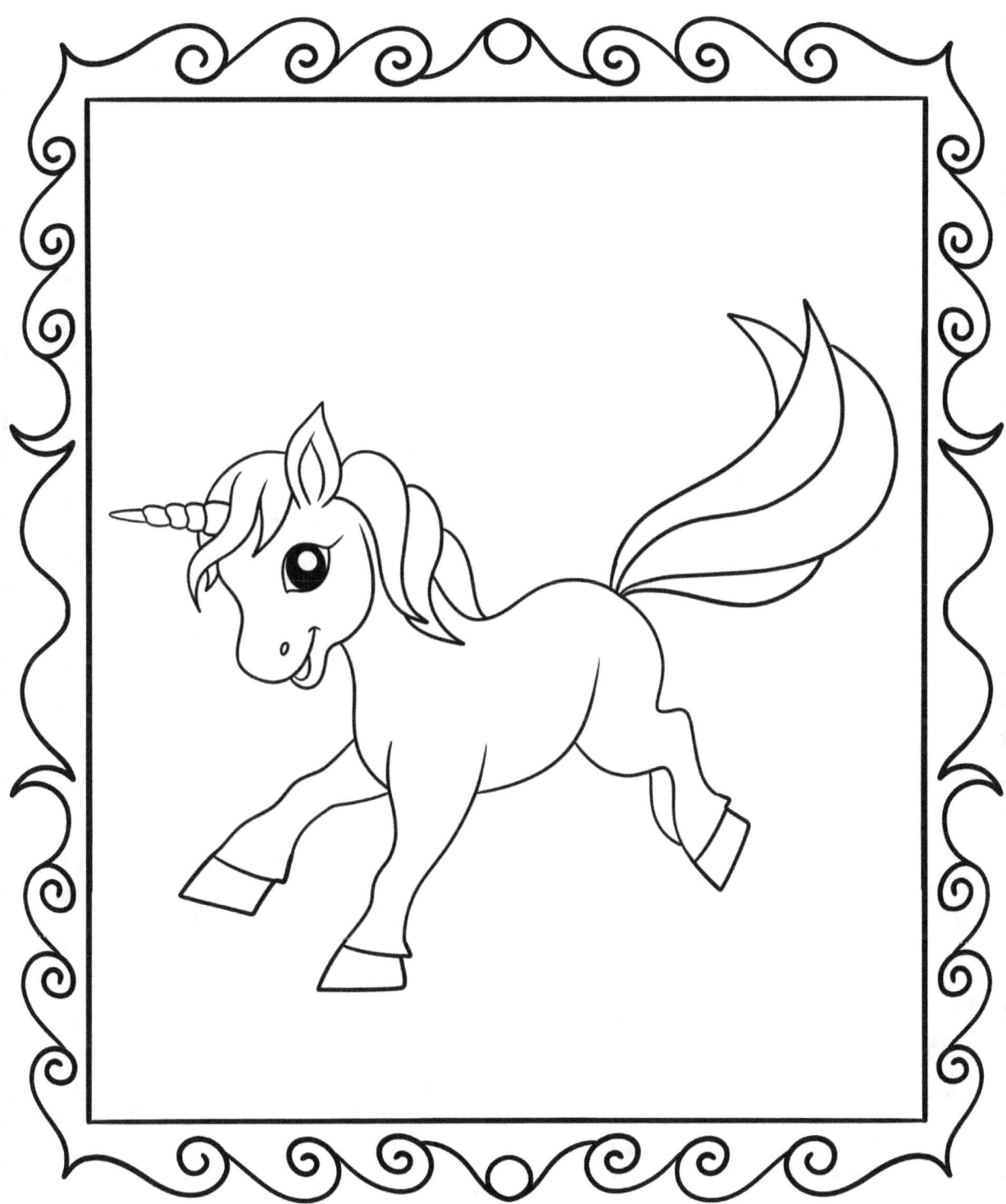

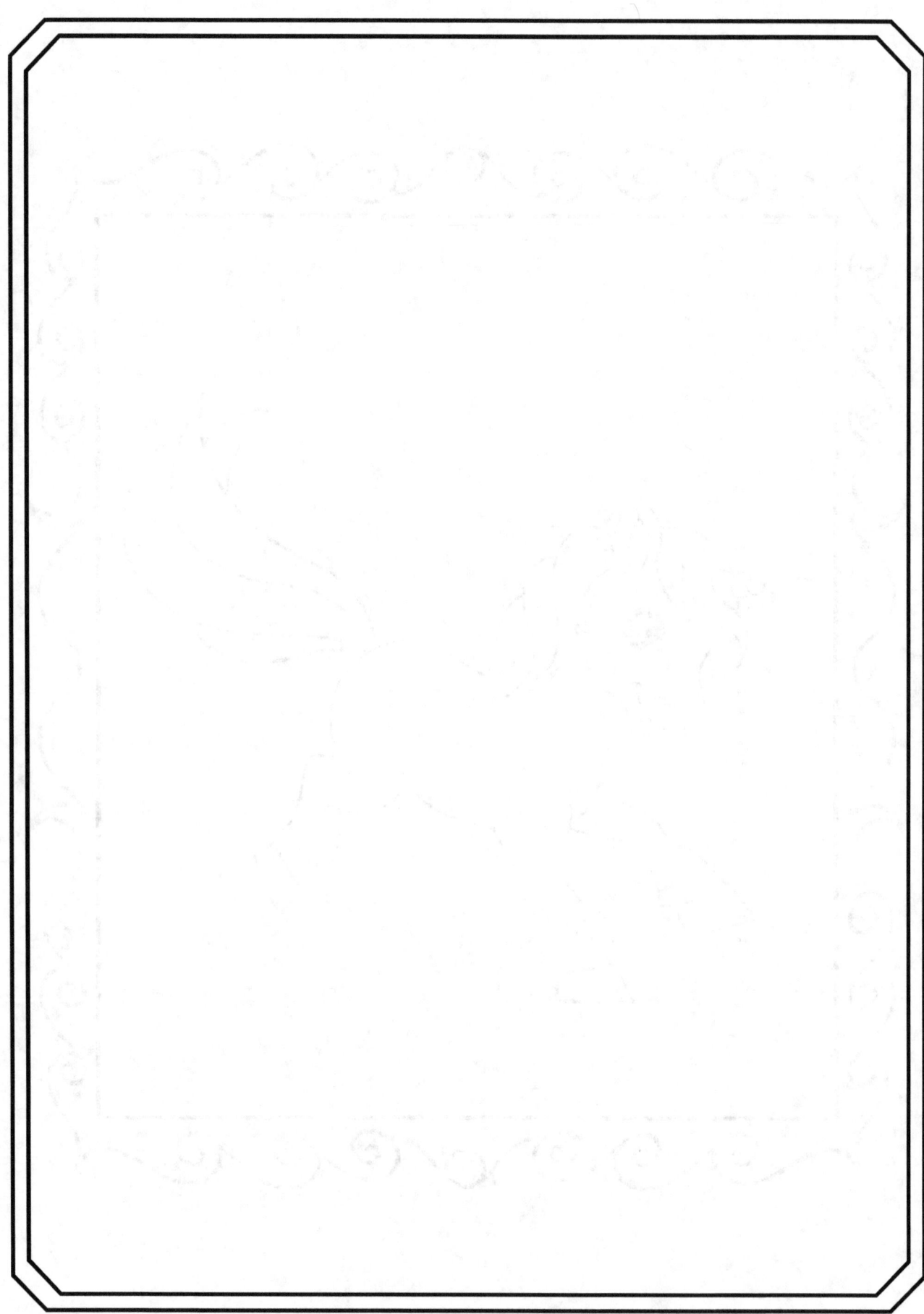

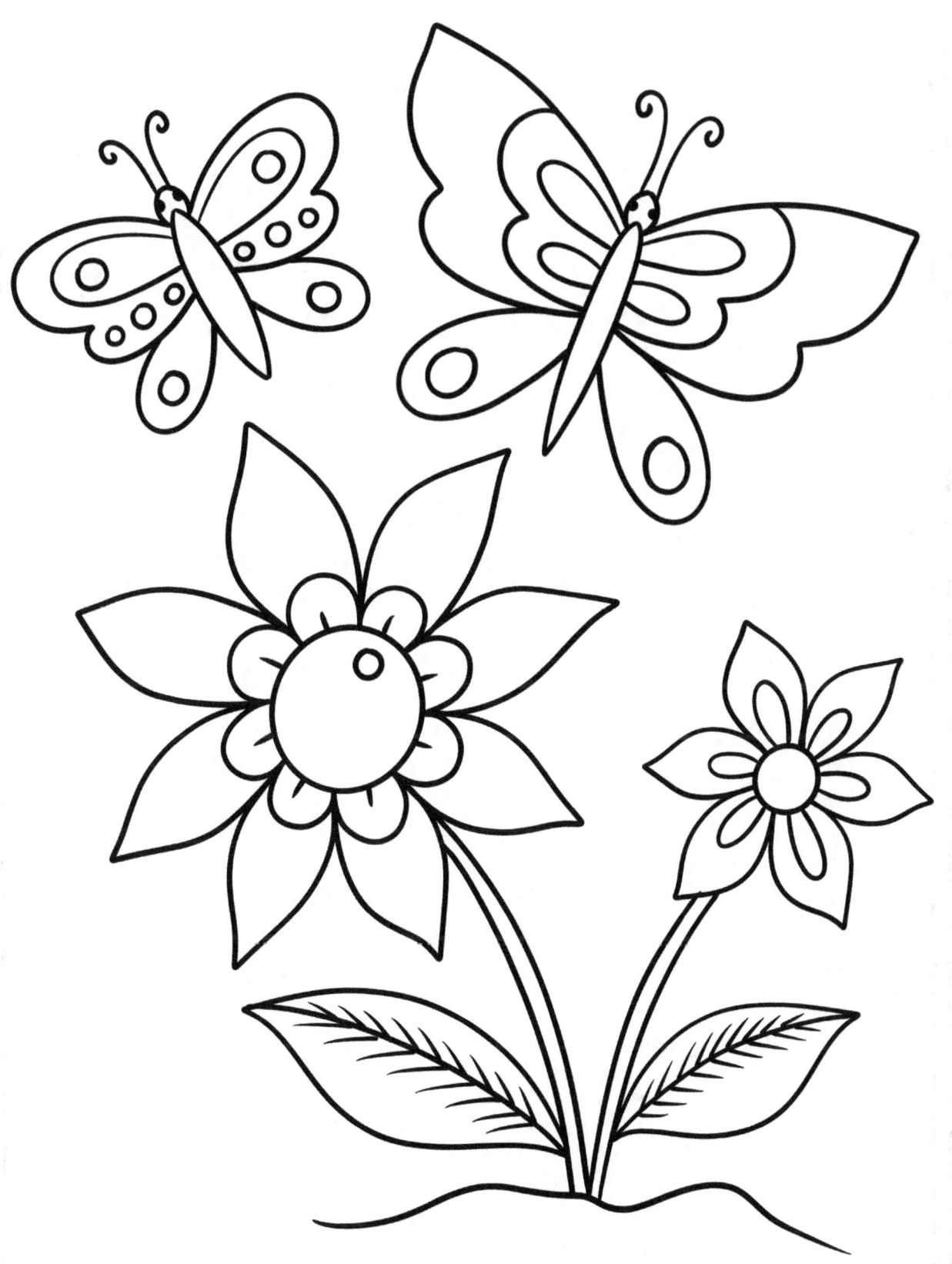

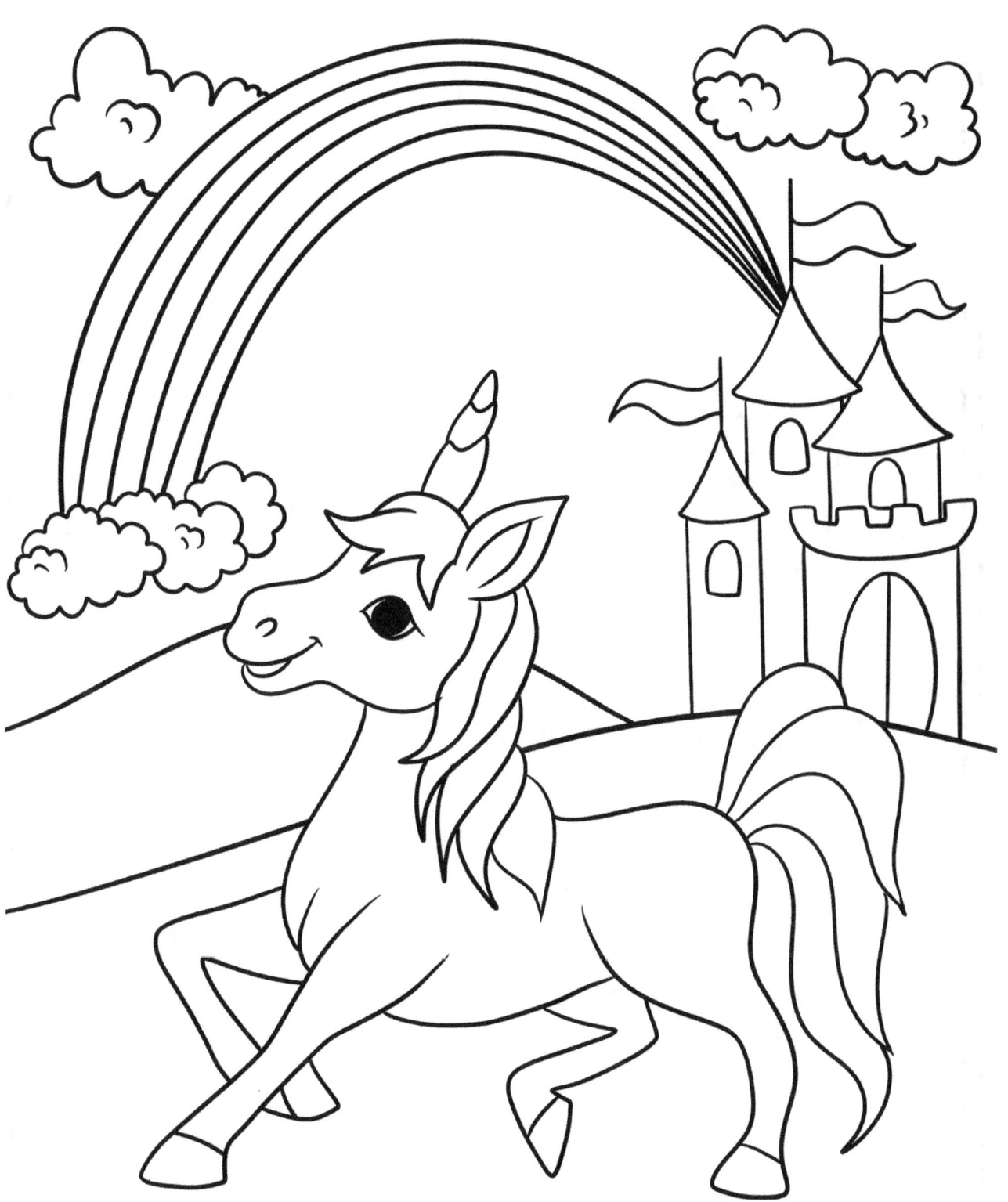

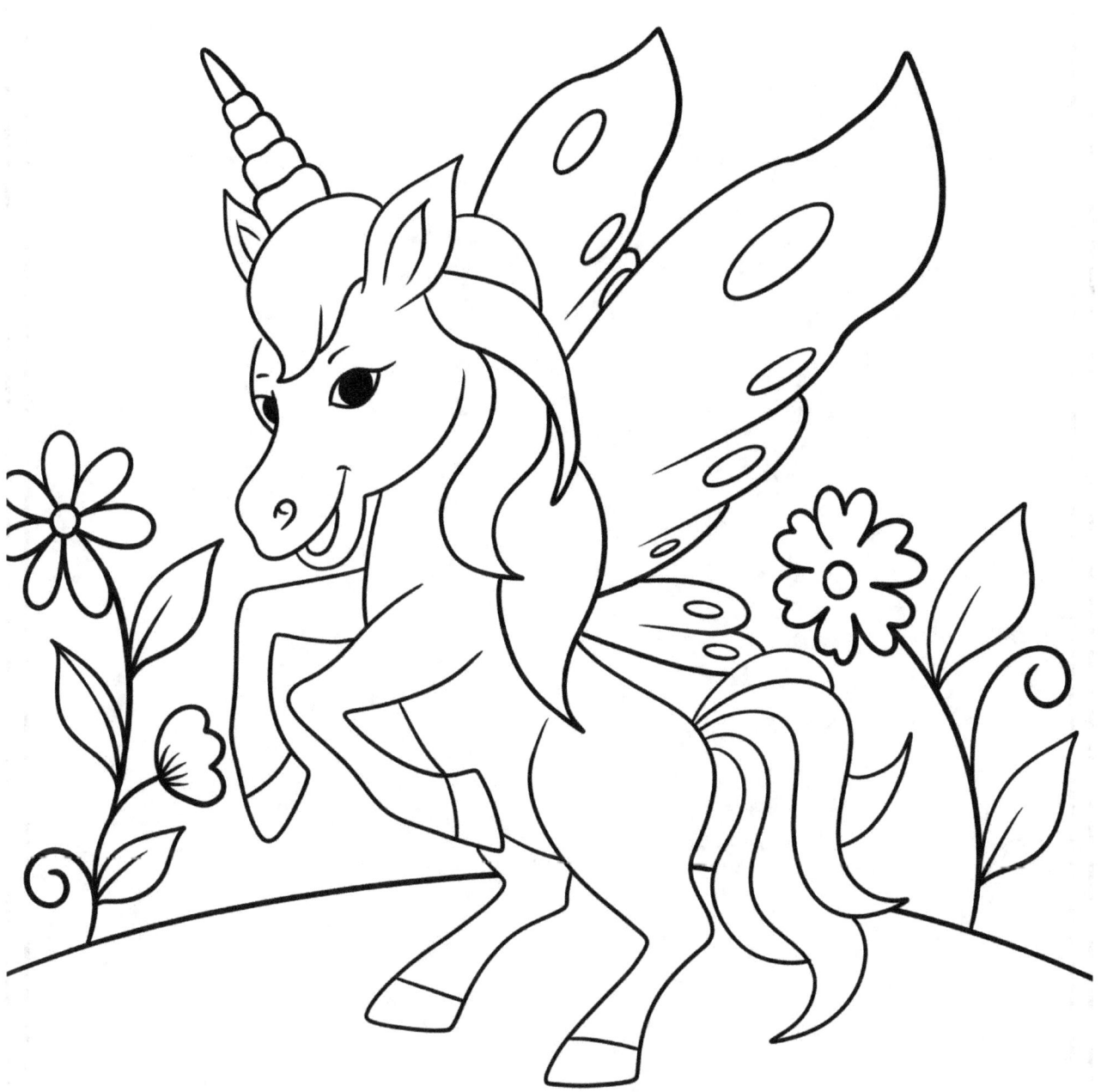

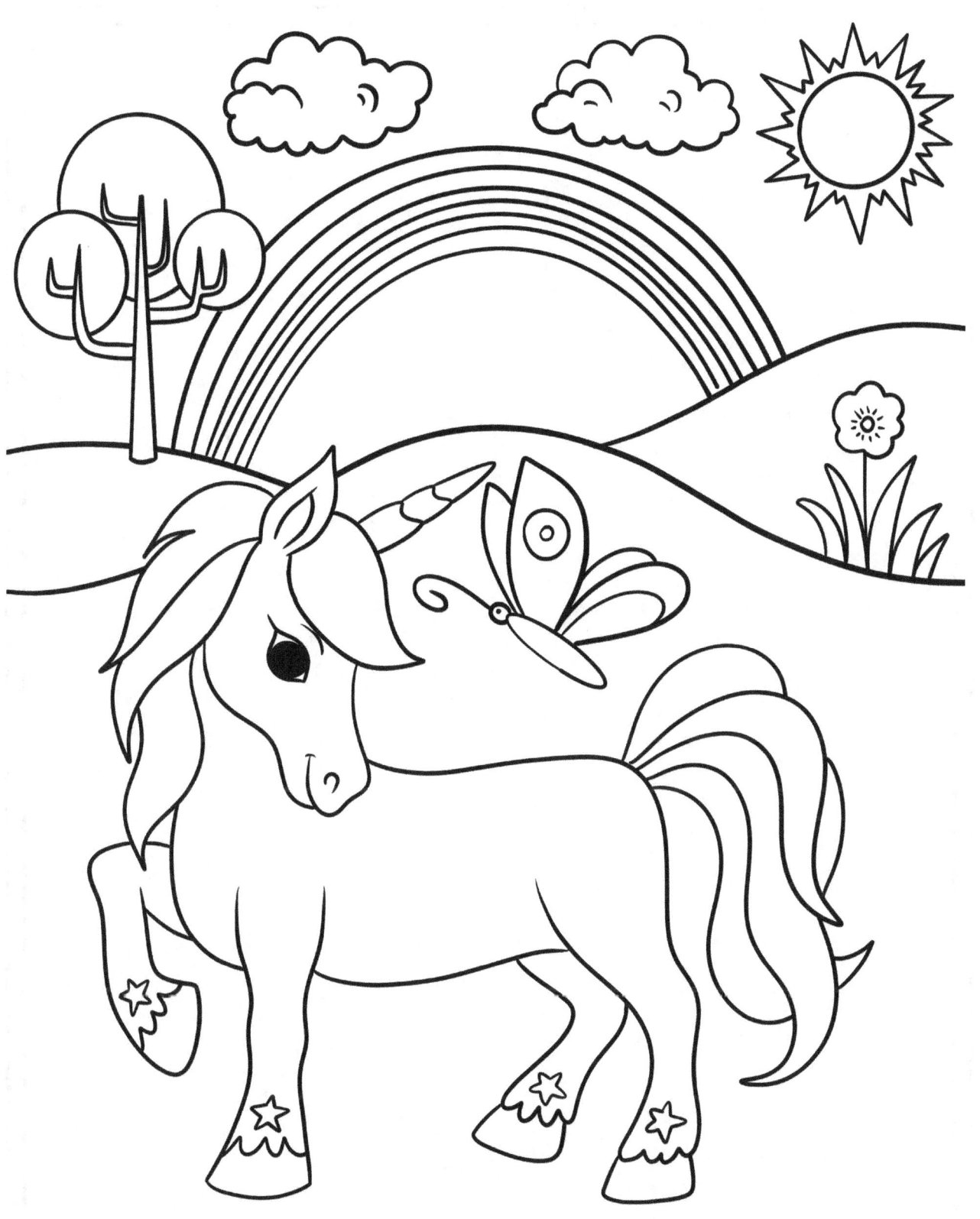

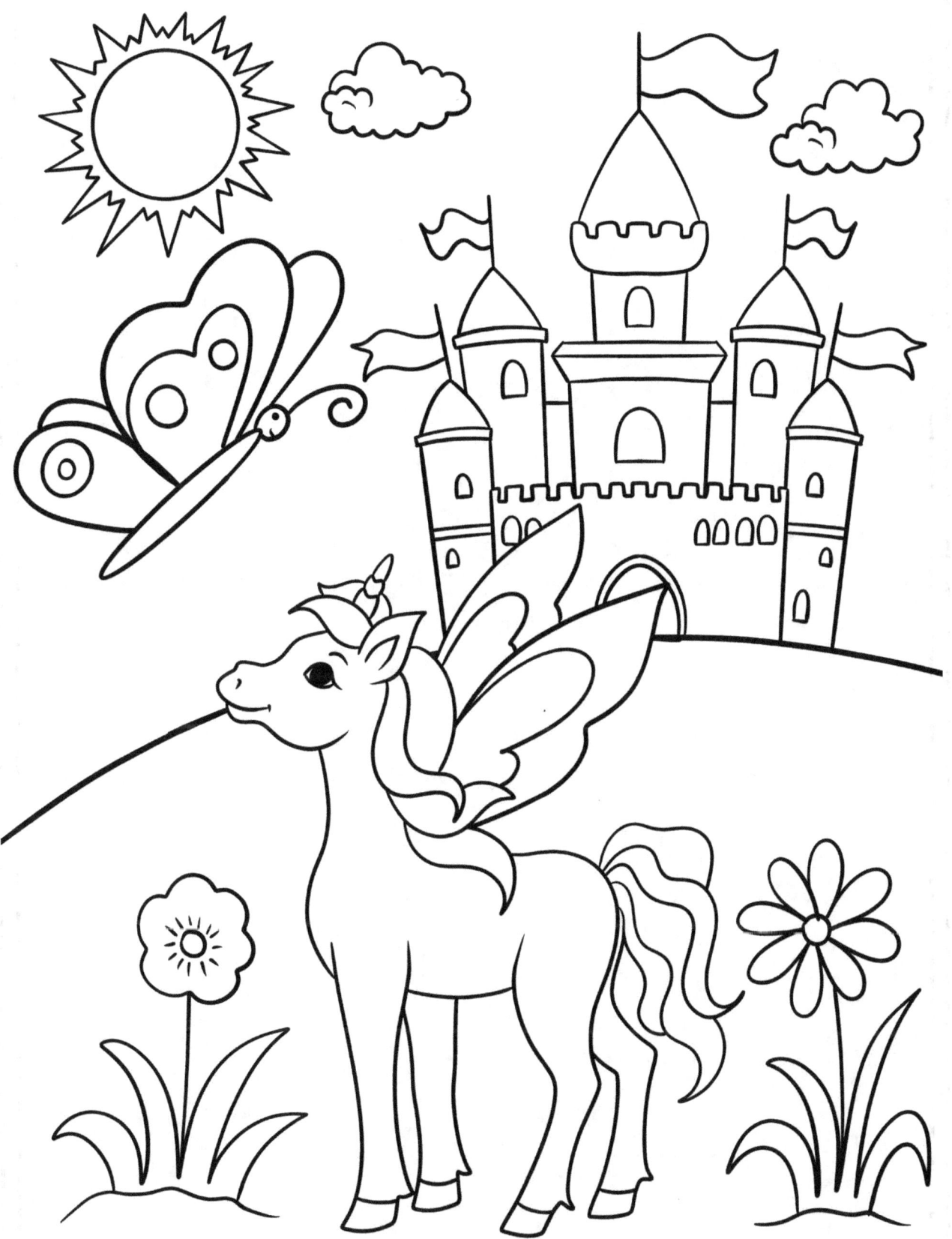

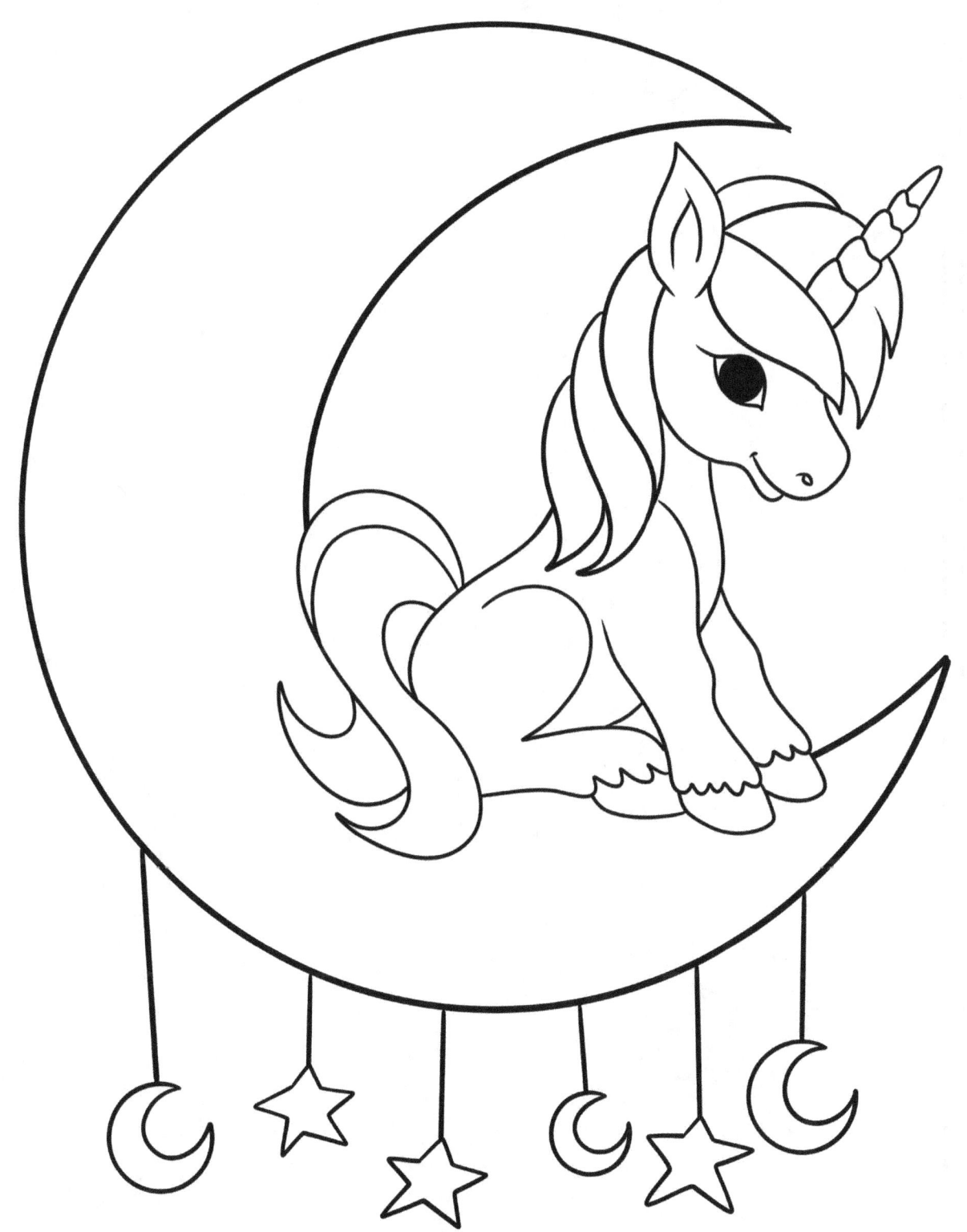

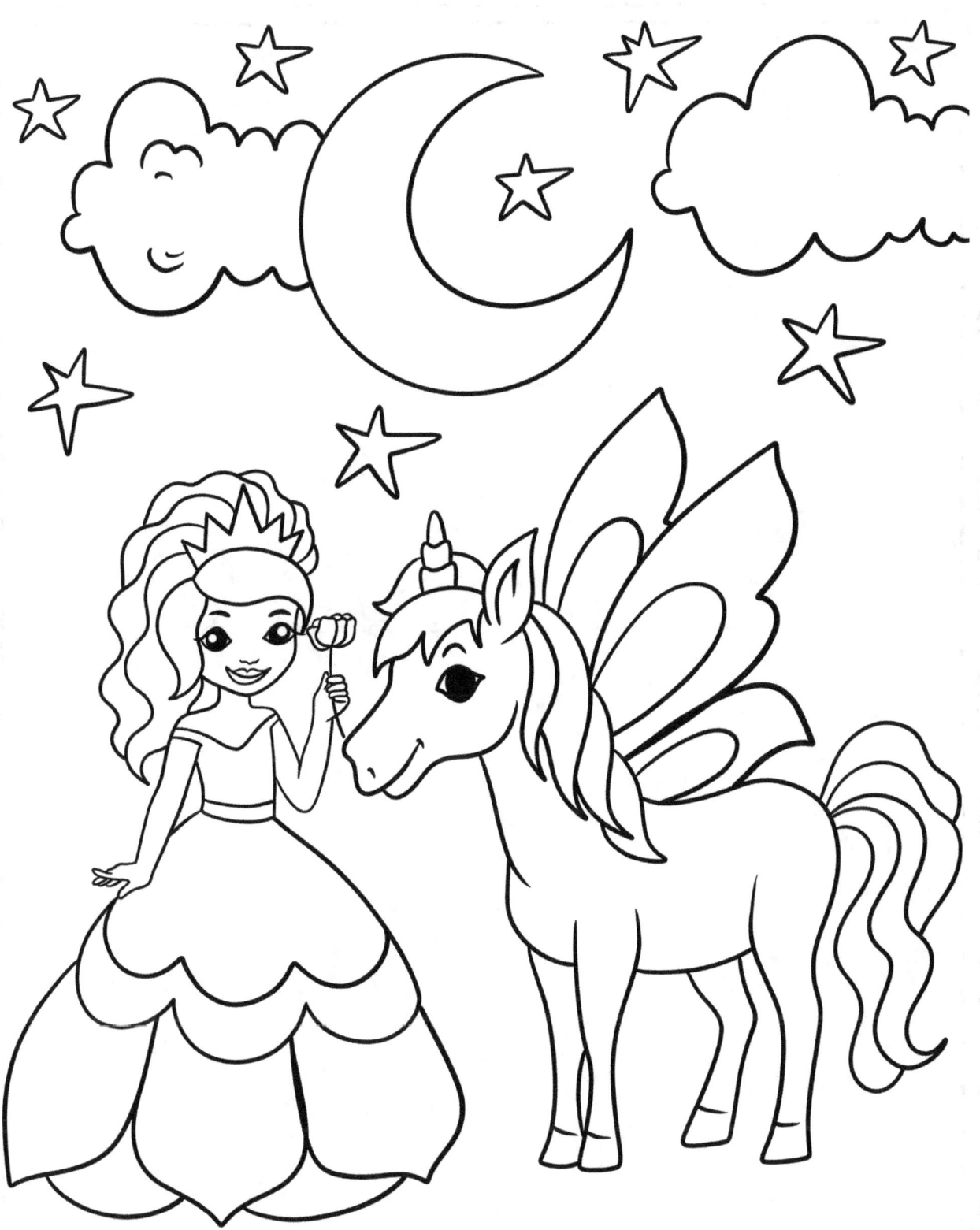

www.ingramcontent.com/pod-product-compliance
Lightning Source LLC
Chambersburg PA
CBHW080530220526
45465CB00006B/2656